BODY OF PRAYER

THE HEAVENS SHALL BE FOLDED TOGETHER AS A BOOK

BODY OF

WRITTEN WORDS

DAVID

MICHAL

JACQUES

PRAYER

VOICES

SHAPIRO

GOVRIN

DERRIDA

THE IRWIN S. CHANIN SCHOOL OF ARCHITECTURE

OF THE COOPER UNION FOR THE ADVANCEMENT OF SCIENCE & ART

KIM SHKAPICH, EDITOR

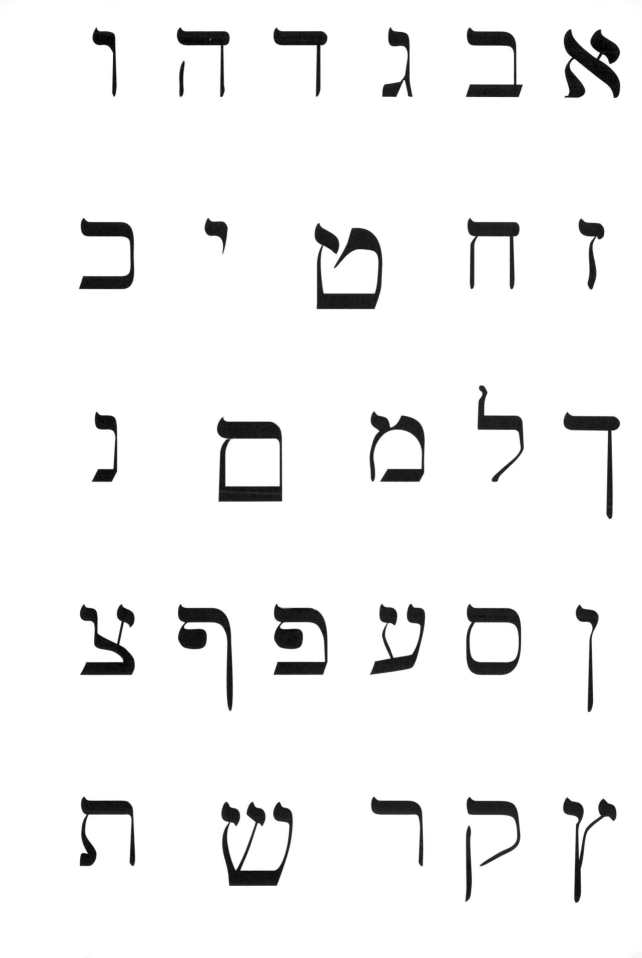

OCTOBER 14 *1998*

B O D Y   O F   P R A Y E R

DAVID SHAPIRO, MICHAL GOVRIN, JACQUES DERRIDA

SHAPIRO

OLD NEW *POEMS*

1:I–IX

WILD PSALM

DAVID SHAPIRO

for Michal Govrin

In another world, listening to a Yemenite dump
Dreaming of Jerusalem our popular flesh,
A sleeper a singer whose name is a triple pun
A language where skin would be light,
It all sounds like the king's first love.
But in this world we sit to translate.
God splits and the blind man's reference
Ends like the war ever not quite.
As we forget the grammar we are of red clay, an idiot.
The supplicants approach, on the field of untranslatable force.
Simone says nothing but: Poetry
More difficult than mathematics, as I warned you.
And the old poets, and the books appear themselves,
Holiness in Sin, that enraged Gershom—the doubled books
And the body's words: Blessed is He who created the creation.
Blessed are they who created the blessing.

OCTOBER 14 *1998*

BODY OF PRAYER

THE DEAD WILL NOT PRAISE YOU

DAVID SHAPIRO

for Cantor Berele Chagy

My grandfather emerges
in a synagogue
with familiar accents
unlike his noble voice
a pudgy little man
sweet tenor coloratura flautando
He marches down the aisle
with a blue white crown
Women ask questions
and they are charmed
and he is beloved
like etymology
Is my mother in attendance
or is she dead?
What are questions now?
Are the dead permitted: to
sing? Is he serious?
Are the dead permitted
to return and sing?

To speak of prayer seems insolent. To think of prayer is perhaps the only serious nostalgia. One remembers that
Kierkegaard and the Talmud prescribe short prayers
against the insolence of rhetorical continuity or bombast.
And Kierkegaard and his Rabbinic colleagues suggest that
we have lost the "true" prayers and can only pray for the
ability to pray, like those paralyzed in the desert without
the nostalgias.[1] A poetics of prayer is no less arrogant, like
the aestheticizing of wonder. Is it for this that Rimbaud
"gave up" poetry? At any rate, we know the taxonomy of
prayer—petition, celebration, meditation, self-laceration,
communion, and thanksgiving—without forgetting
Kant's aversion to the grovelling religions. We discrimi-
nate tonight, so that we can think even of that strange
structure, the prayer without addressee. It is not for nothing that we bring together Jacques Derrida, the Jewish
poet in his extreme free fall, the golden voice against
excessive voice, and a student of Lévinas's sense of the
naked face of the Other, and Michal Govrin, who has
described the space of intense prayer in her prose, poetry,
and theater. The Irwin S. Chanin School of Architecture of
the Cooper Union welcomes this night's meditation on
the body of prayer.

    The prayer-book in the Jewish tradition, the hymns
that inflected the dark poet Emily Dickinson, the utterly
mesmerizing couplets of the Angelus Silesius—these are
musical boundaries. The clarity of the tradition of the
Psalms, for example, or of Rumi's whirling couplets, is a
clarity of the paradox of speaking of the unspeakable. Is it
for this that Wittgenstein, for a while, gave up philosophy,
or perhaps forever? Is it for this that the ladder we can
throw away of his propositions has been described as a
rungless ladder, or one we could not climb? The philosopher in jail feels the daemon requires him to learn the
flute, or is that musical prayer? It is a sudden urge for the
body of a *niggun*, perhaps, the wordless tune by which
prayer enters, again and again, the dithyrambic urges of
the Hasids. We know and might know now that prayer
consists of a encyclopedic palette of unknowing: *para-
doxia epidemica*. In this oxymoronic tradition, "we" are the

DAVID SHAPIRO

1
PERRY D. LEFEVRE,
PRAYERS OF
KIERKEGAARD
(CHICAGO:
UNIVERSITY OF
CHICAGO PRESS,
1956), 202.

WALTER BENJAMIN: A LOST POEM

DAVID SHAPIRO

after a dream

In a lost essay on poetry, Walter Benjamin had written, *I was born into a rich, perhaps too rich and too comfortable existence in Berlin. Each time my family saw soot in the air we wanted to move to another vacation spot. Poetry today withholds too much. What does it withhold. At any rate, eclecticism, Prokofiev . . .* The most Brechtian poem of Benjamin has almost been forgotten. It was published under the title *David*, with a section of a door knob as a slightly Duchampian typographic oddity. I found the proofs, rare as the Redon for *A Throw of the Dice*, in a bookstore. The poem was fairly simple:

> David or King David
> How
> did you
> done
> your door

Unfortunately, many of Benjamin's remarks on poetry were now simple scratches on the cover of the book, effaced like the infamous magic writing pad and indecipherable as hidden love (as opposed to open rebuke). Some of his lost short stories appear in this volume. Scholem said, There was nothing like being alone with Walter Benjamin. *It made one want to read.* The source of that remark is also lost.

community of saints, struggling with a diction that can hardly exceed ourselves. Monsieur Derrida has been one of the most stringent of all those readers who have led us to think of the opacities of our linguistic contradictions and excesses. Govrin has found in the concrete laws of temporary shelter a sacred architecture. And she has also proposed the dangers of those falling upwards into prayer in the City of Prayer, fought over, as she has proposed canonically, like a woman (or The Spirit).

John Hejduk draws angels and draws like an angel. He has averred that his whole life he has been creating houses and houses of worship. He said, "Actually houses are houses of worship." This morning our acting associate dean and student of John Hejduk told me "each house is a prayer." The analogical notions may seem too abundant for those who reject LeFebre's claim that all architecture has an "acoustic" element.

In Hejduk's recent extreme poetry, Christ, Braque, and Rodin meet and mingle in a Borgesian wallpaper. In Govrin's new novel *The Name/HaShem*, a woman rises and sinks into a variety of cults and exposes a whole extreme history to test the integrity of a praying body. In recent books on Lévinas and justice, Jacques Derrida seems also willing to come perilously close to what we must describe as a commitment to hopeless prayer. Elsewhere, Michal Govrin has admitted that for her Kaballah does not end but includes our contemporary and tenebrous divigations. As one grows older, one cannot accept our prayer-book without Proust and Kafka, those who have best added to our sense of the starry disorder within and the starry chaos outside. We welcome the philosopher of doubt and the novelist of space here together as parts of a stichomythia concerning what is a dialogue in the eschatological scene of prayer.

Monsieur Derrida has come from his classes. We'll leave him alone so it could be like a silent prayer, which is one of the mysteries of the grammar of prayer, for me, the voiceless prayer or the prayer inside and so he may or may not speak.

I'm going to test to the fact that the prayer is silent.   JACQUES DERRIDA

THE BOSS POEM

DANIEL SHAPIRO

with David Shapiro

Are you the boss of God?
You are the boss of God?
Nobody is the boss of God
Not me not you
Are the angels the boss of God?
Are you more famous than angels?
God is the boss of Himself
Orders Himself
To do what he wants
I am the boss of this poem
I wrote it

As a kind of framing I'm just going to read one of JOHN HEJDUK'S poems. I like the idea in terms of the grammar of prayer, that he's both with us and not.

NIGHT SON

blood snow
overflowing
music silenced
death's circle

sin confession
helpless
to disappeared

where art thou

bucolic landscape
ripped
smoke filled earth
shovel after shovel

to outlive
a mother's murder
dare organs sound
again
mixing language into
unable forgetfulness

my son
I cannot
hear you
any longer

evaporating Jerusalem

HERE

absorbing
crystal
lines
black

hard
cries
forsaken

there

afire
torn
nobreath
emptied

night
nomercy
ever
given
no
speechless

my son
I cannot
hear you
any longer

here

A POEM FOR
PAUL CELAN
DEDICATED TO
MICHAL GOVRIN

And, as just one other part of the framing device, I am going to read this prayer and then Michal will speak.

LIGHT BULB

DAVID SHAPIRO

1960

Our father
restless afraid of death
would say You will rest
when you're dead

Perhaps not!
And: Practice or you'll eat
in the garage
with the dog

Dead as the light
bulb is living still
A secret for the light bulb
is the nap

of broken music
There are some veins
in brown plaster
But the world emits

a little light
You wore cereal boxes
as a belt
I wore electric light

as another mistake
The search continued
for more veins and
a dented skull

This too had a pedestal
or place
or base or double
door or triple tomb.

PRAYER FOR A HOUSE

Blessed is the architect of the removed structures
Blessed is the structure that weathers in spring snow like lies
Blessed is the crystal that leaps out of the matrix like a fool
And blessed is the school

Blessed factures
Blessed like spring snow
Blessed like a fool
And burnt book

FOR JOHN HEJDUK

Is the school a structure or weather
Or a lie like spring snow
And is the matrix leaping also like a fool
And is the book built or burnt?

Blessed is the removed
Blessed too the inlay like spring
Blessed is the tiger of the matrix like a found fool
And blessed the unbuilt like a book

Blessed is the architect who survives all removal
Blessed is the trapped structure like a gift
Blessed is the crystal fool
And blessed is the school

Blessed is the cut and the cry
Blessed the body of the patient in spring snow like lies
Blessed is the crystal stepping out of the matrix like a fool
And blessed is a burning book

Blessed is the anchorite and the architect in the dark smudge
Blessed is the remover bending to remove
Blessed is the folly leaping out of matrix
And blessed is the empty center

Blessed burning structures
Blessed like snowy spring
Blessed cry blessed in the matrix like a cut fool
And blessed each unlit book

Blessed is the architect of the removed cut
Blessed the structures that weather in lies like spring snow
Blessed is the crystal that leaps out of the matrix like a fool
And blessed is the school, like a burning library

Old new prayer
Old new song
Blessed is the crystal and the cry and the matrix like a painting fool
And blessed is the school

WINTER WORK

DAVID SHAPIRO

A dog prays.
      For me.
He barks inside all day, what little inside there is, like a pigeon.
Help!
He kneels for his king one night
Kind owner. "Ayeka?" All is kind,
      All is cruel.
A dog's prayed, obeyed, spayed.
In the forest now, he moans for help
In some of his languages. No one!
The addressee slips away,
Has slipped away.
But a dog thinks.
The dog thanks you in the desert.
In the desert
Of the desert, you have left a trace.

I am going to speak while I sit so I hope that you can hear me. I think that my voice will build up from the silence and the emotions. My voice is a little choked, especially since I have to speak in public, pray in public, perform in public in front of you today, which is for me a very moving moment to be here with you and surrounded the way I am. As we just heard the blessings, I must put in words what the blessing of being here is for me, and I hope that this blessing is not only personal but that it propagates. To be invited and to come to the Cooper Union over the last nine years—every fall when I am in this continent for a short time—has provided a tremendous space of inspiration and experimentation. The most audacious possible, always crossing unknown spaces.

MICHAL GOVRIN

The encounter with John Hejduk's books, ideas, the space he created here. This constant daring of going beyond the given structure. As a novelist, you deal so much with the architecture of meaning, of language, the way you build it, walk through it. I think Cooper Union is one of the great schools questioning the architecture of narrative. My novel *The Name/HaShem* is structured as a prayer, a prayer which emerges from the point of destruction, from the point of the wound, of the holocaust. I know of few works that open as powerfully as John Hejduk's *Victims*, with the question of memory. An incredible meditation about a monument for a buried shout, a place for memory which is as mobile, as organic as the human memory, and has in it a narrative of the people who cross its space, like a novel, like a poem, and like a building. I have been marked by Hejduk's deeply human and humanistic work, and by the unique work which is done here at Cooper Union.

I am very grateful to Jacques Derrida for being here, I don't know how he has the energy to join us, which is beyond the energy of the average performer; but also because it's an opportunity to privately and publicly, thank him for the inspiration over all those years.

A MONUMENT

DAVID SHAPIRO

for Michal Govrin

temporary
rainbow—
temporary dove—
valid—
a raven with
no leaf—
that is
a dove
or wall
citron or
dispute—
permanent—
thorn—palms from
the Iron Mountains—
the present ovelapped
with angel's wings—
valid—
whale's skin
bad memory of—
old story Leviathan—
over a perishable
house of holes
over the good
enough ark
OVER A FLOOD
OF CLOUDS

While writing I was conversing constantly with "the
Jewish text"—this breathtaking archeological site of
books from the Bible, through the Talmud to contemporary writings with their myriad of perspectives. I tried
to excavate hidden voices, to unravel forgotten myths,
to read them in another way, yes, to deconstruct them.
And as for the prayer: isn't there, at the core of prayer, a
deep gesture of deconstruction, an effort to shatter con-
gealed or deadened forms, not in order to discard them,
but in order to reactivate the bursting voice. Something
that might be called, a "prayer from the ashes." An image
that always haunted me within Jacques Derrida's writings and which I always felt so close at heart.

And David, do I know someone else whose whole
existence is a prayer and a blessing to the others? This
always open hand to invite, to see, to listen, to meet
other people. I think of David as a walking example of
ethics, and to say it in a more humoristic way, I think he
is my Jewish pal on the other side of the ocean; and we
converse—overseas conversations about Rosenzweig,
or Benjamin—how many people you can do that with?
And then the luxury and the opportunity and blessing
of being invited here, to David's classes. And his violin,
that reverberates, through the novel, since that night
when he called, and with an incredible gesture of gen-
erosity, rushed, picked up his violin and played over the
phone, so beautifully. David didn't know that at that
time I was searching for the words that could echo the
tone of the violin. That night over the long distance call
he gave me the tone.

Preparing this talk these last days, thinking about
prayer in order to speak here, in this specific locale, this
topos here, The Cooper Union, engendered a totally different thinking for me. So, a novel built as a prayer. A
prayer uttered during the novel, and becoming its dura-
tion, building it. Building and prayer. Isn't praying like
being inside a building while building it? Planning,
making the sketches, from within. Building without

MICHAL GOVRIN

PSALM

DAVID SHAPIRO

Lord, I am not too happy.
I am not looking too high.
I am not wasting my time
        on the marvelous, too marvelous for me.
My mind is calm and quiet
like a quiet child on the breast;
my mind is like that quiet child.

Israel, you must hope
now and always.

any distance, without ever encompassing the totality of the space, but losing oneself inside it, and with total abnegation, advancing with an inevitable necessity. Preparing for today, I was leafing through the pages of the Talmud, treatise Blessings [Berachot], Chapter Five, the central jewish text where the question of "how to pray" is debated. I have already read these pages I don't know how many times, and still, every reading is another understanding, another unfolding…. This time a forgotten small sentence caught my eye:

MICHAL GOVRIN

A PERSON SHOULD ALWAYS PRAY IN A HOUSE WITH WINDOWS. [2]

2
TALMUD,
BERACHOT, 31A.

I leave you with this image, of prayer in a house with windows. Here, at The Cooper Union.

This morning at five o'clock I woke up from the rain and the storm and all of a sudden I remembered the very first time when I felt the need to have a prayer book. Suddenly a whole other layer came back to me. As if a forgotten window was open. You should know that I grew up in a totally secular home, as they say. (*Totally secular* is an oxymoron when you speak about Israeli reality. Nothing is ever totally secular in Israel). Let's say I grew up in a non-observant home, where the prayer book had a cultural value but was never *used*. No one prayed at home. At least not in a canonical manner. Not with prayer books. If there were prayers, they took on other forms. Like, for me, the shock of discovering Kafka at an early age. My parents had their forms of prayer, not less powerful. My father's deeply Hasidic intense attentiveness, or, my mother's ongoing account with the Unspeakable, so palpable on Yom Kippur, in the defiant silence that enveloped her when she didn't get out of bed the whole day. Breaking away from the tradition was a strong and complex statement. Later, away from home, and away from Israel with its loaded narrative,

SARCOPHAGUS FOR THE SILENCE OF GOD

DAVID SHAPIRO

for John Hejduk and Picard

Sarcophagus for the still small voice
Sarcophagus for the marriage of truth and troth
Sarcophagus for the mother of the hypocritical poet
Sarcophagus for the lava of speech
                              the incline of music
Sarcophagus for the materials for the messiah without melancholy

Sarcophagus for the misidentified corpse of the architect
Sarcophagus for the flower beyond flowers
Sarcophagus for the suicidal architect for the hand on the edge
Sarcophagus for the powerless computer for the traditional book
Sarcophagus for the one fairy tale

Sarcophagus for the future tense and for the subjunctive in the
gloom
          of the miracle for Thomas Hardy's ox-cart man
Sarcophagus for the twins of frozen speech and for the luminous
                    sounds of the surface
Sarcophagus for the slave of writing crying help in all
          languages for wild sound for the twins of frozen speech
Sarcophagus for the mistranslators

during my Ph.D. studies in Paris, I felt an urge, almost   MICHAL GOVRIN
physical, to do some gestures, "Jewish gestures". The
body always came before the thought. The need to *be*,
before understanding *why*. So, at that time I started to
eat kosher which was an acrobatic performance in Paris,
and started in a very personal way to mark the weekly
space of Sabbath. And then, in 1975 and I was a very
young student, I had an urge to travel to Poland. An
urge which I did not fully understand at that time.
There were no diplomatic relationships between Israel
and Poland and I sneaked in for seven days with the
alibi that I represented France in a certain vague theater festival that I left the day I arrived, to go on my *real*
trip. Before leaving for Poland I went to a synagogue
that I knew, the synagogue at Rue Michel-Ange which
housed the school that Emmanuel Lévinas headed and
I partly asked, partly purloined a prayer book. I felt I
needed it embarking on that trip, to my mother's past,
to the place where she lost her first husband and son,
where she was incarcerated. I was traveling all alone,
before there were organized tours, or collective identi-
ties of "children of the second generation"; traveling
without prepared words, without language. I used the
prayer book once, when the dizziness was unbearable,
and only ancient words could hold me. In the "museum"
at Auschwitz where my mother was an inmate, before
she was sent on the Death March to Bergen-Belsen.
There, in front of the pile of shoes, as if it were a *place*, I
took out the prayer book and recited the *Kaddish*, for the
first time in my life. I started to write *The Name* shortly
after this journey, a novel that found itself being written in the form of the prayer. I don't think that I knew
why I did it. Somehow, I decided with an urge, a body
urge, that I wanted to pray, or at least pray the way I
knew. And the only way I knew was through writing.
The memory that came back this morning was putting
the prayer at the place where it originated for me. What
I understood, coming here today, was that this writing,

JOURNEY TO POLAND *WITH LETTER*
2:I–XXV

in a way, was a Proustian *A la recherche du temps perdu*, but *after* the Holocaust, when the lost memory is far from being an idyllic one. The writing became a research into a concealed identity hidden within the character, her memory, her body-memory: traces of a buried shout, of a buried, suffocated prayer.

I am very embarrassed to speak about my own work. I pretend as if I am at ease but it's an extremely difficult performance, so permit me to insert a reading and I'll go from there. For those who know, and for those who don't know maybe I'll start with a few lines in Hebrew that you'll just hear the flavor, the body of language.

בע"ה
היום תשעה ימים שהם שבוע אחד ושני ימים לעומר.
גבורה שבגבורה.

יהי רצון מלפניך ה' אלוקי ואלוקי אבותי
שבזכות ספירת העומר שספרתי היום יתוקן מה
שפגמתי בספירה גבורה שבגבורה, ואטהר ואתקדש
בקדושה של מעלה. ועל-ידי זה יושפע שפע רב בכל
העולמות לתקן את נפשותינו ורוחותינו ונשמותינו
מכל סיג ופגם, ולטהרנו ולקדשנו בקדושתך העליונה.
אמן סלה.
יהי רצון מלפניך ה' אלוקי ואלוקי אבותי שתבוא
לפניך תפילתי. כי אתה שומע תפילת כל פה.
שתקבלני באהבה וברצון. שיהא מיעוט חלבי-ודמי,
שנתמעט היום, כחלב מונח על גבי המיזבח לפניך.
ותרצני.

Before reading from the wonderful translation of Barbara Harshav let me point out the special status of the "I" in the prayer. At the outburst of every new prayer there is always an "I" pouring out his utmost intimacy. Yet, once this outpour—a chapter of Psalms, for example —turns into "a prayer", it becomes public, and is taken over by other voices, becoming their most intimate "I". Who says "I" when I read? The Kabbalist who put together the quoted prayer; the character, Amalia; Barbara Harshav, whose I is embodied in the English, or

MICHAL GOVRIN

MICHAL GOVRIN

TRANSLATED
FROM THE
HEBREW BY
BARBARA
HARSHAV

In late October 1975, when I was in my early twenties and completing my doctorate in Paris, I went to Poland. An almost impossible journey then for a young woman, alone, with an Israeli passport, at the time when there were no diplomatic relations between the Eastern Bloc and Israel. It was only because of a French-Jewish friend, who turned me into a "Representative of France" at the International Theater Festival in Wroclaw [Breslau], that I received a special visa for a week.

The night before the trip, when everything was ready, I called my parents in Tel Aviv and told them. I asked my shocked mother for the exact address of her family home in Kraków. Only later that winter, when I visited Israel, did I understand what profound emotion took hold of my mother's few surviving friends and relatives from Kraków when they heard of the trip.

A week later I returned to Paris. For twenty-four hours, I closed myself in my student apartment in the Latin Quarter, far from the Parisian street scenes, and feverishly wrote to my parents. A letter of more then twenty pages. First thoughts, a summary of the rapid notes taken on the trip. Even the words groped for another language, for a different level of discourse.

That year, as every year, a commemoration for the Jewish community of Kraków was held in the auditorium of my high school in Tel Aviv. News of my trip and of that letter reached the members of the community, and they wanted to read it aloud at that commemoration. I agreed, and after it was commandeered from the family circle, I submitted it for publication to the literary supplement of the newspaper, *Davar*, with the title, "Letter from Regions of Delusion" (the expression Regions of Delusion was borrowed from the title, given by Martin Buber, to a parable of Rabbi Israel Ba'al Shem Tov, the founder of Hasidism). Aside from some peripheral changes of style, that text appears here.

Traveling in Poland in 1975 was not part of the social phenomenon it is today. The group definition of "second-generation Holocaust survivors" hadn't yet been coined. You had to

myself, as I read here in front of you, which is maybe another form of praying? The extreme case of prayer reminds us how much the "I" is shattered, as we always say I in more than one way, we are always more that one I.

WITH THE HELP OF GOD...TODAY IS NINE DAYS, WHICH IS ONE WEEK AND TWO DAYS OF THE OMER. POWER OF POWER.

The book opens with a quote from a prayer said at the Counting of the Omer, the forty-nine days between Passover and Shavuoth, between Exodus and the reception of the Torah on Mount Sinai. This passage, the time frame of *The Name*, is marked every year as a mystical crescendo and lived with intensity. So, I start again:

WITH THE HELP OF GOD...TODAY IS NINE DAYS, WHICH IS ONE WEEK AND TWO DAYS OF THE OMER. POWER OF POWER.

May it be your will, HaShem, Holy Name, my God and God of my fathers, that in the merit of the Omer Count that I have marked today, there may be corrected whatever blemish I have made in the Sefirah Power of Power. May I be cleansed and sanctified with the Holiness of Above, and through this may abundant bounty flow in all the worlds. And may it correct our lives, our spirits, our souls from all sediment and blemish, may it cleanse us and sanctify us with Your exalted holiness.

Amen!

May it be your will, HaShem, Holy Name, my God and God of my fathers, that my prayer come before Thee. For You hear the prayer of each mouth.

May You accept me with love and desire. May my little bit of fat and blood diminished today be as fat placed on the altar before You. And may You want me.

If only it could end here. If only my sacrifice were complete, and my expiation full before I finish the task. May You at night force my hands to completion, as I shall attempt in the day to complete the holy task of weaving. *To You and to You.* With devotion.

find out everything by yourself. How to plan the trip and how to feel, how to talk about it. The letter to my parents as the addressees of an intimate discourse was not the norm then.

Today, that trip seems like a geological rift that changed my emotional and intellectual landscape, and placed its seal on my writing. Yet the "journey to Poland" didn't begin in 1975, but in early childhood, in Tel Aviv in the 1950s. Distant shocks preceded the rift.

The journey to Poland began in that journey *to there*—the journey every child makes to the regions of before he was born, to the unknown past of his parents, to the secret of his birth. My journey to Mother's world began long before I "understood" who my mother, Regina Rina Poser-Laub-Govrin, was, before I "knew" that she survived the Holocaust, that she once had another husband, that I had a half-brother. But there was the other "knowledge," that knowledge of pre-knowledge and pre-language, transmitted in the thousand languages that connect a child and his parents without words. A knowledge that lay like a dark cloud on the horizon. Terrifying and seductive.

For years the journey proceeded on a double track. One outside the home and one inside it. And there was an almost complete separation between the two. As if everything that was said outside had nothing to do with Mother. Outside, incomprehensible, violent stories about the "Holocaust" were forced upon the little girl's consciousness. In school assemblies, in lessons for Holocaust Memorial Day, and later on in lessons of "Annals of the Jewish People," which were taught separately from "history" classes, and described events that happened in "another, Jewish time and place," where King David and small-town Jews strolled among the goats and railroad cars of the ghetto. Even the Eichmann Trial, on the radio in school and at home, was an event you had to listen to, but it had no real relation to Mother. (And even if things were said about it then at home, I succeeded in repressing them from consciousness.)

At home, there were bright stories about Kraków, the boulevards, the Hebrew high school, the cook, the maids, about skiing and summer holidays in the mountains, in Zakopane, and some-

When the pages are opened from their binding, my soul will be one with the weave of the Torah Curtain. A blue sky of secrets and woven silk bindings. Your kiss.

Another forty days. And the body is already burning in Your fire.

Another forty days. To lead the end of the thread, back and forth, to wind it around the slabs of the spools, to empty it sheaf by sheaf on the warp beam, to thread it string by string through the eyes of the rake, the eyes of the thresher, the comb, the tracks, to tie it tightly, loop by loop, between the frame of the loom. Another forty days to pass cord by cord the plaiting of the woof in the trembling of the warp. Another forty days at last, with outstretched arms. Toward You. Body to body and breath to breath.

The night is dim. And the big vaulted room, too, is almost completely dark. I've placed the table next to the window, and we are surrounded only by the ring of light from the single lamp. The rest of the room is here and not here. Better like that. Stronger. The Torah Curtain is hung, warp threads empty and stretched from side to side across the back of the loom; its murmur is coming up here, blending with the thin rustle of dust rising from the desert and scattering on the stones of the sill, on the lintel of the window. And around me, on the table, the pages. And in the cabinet, the closed boxes of photographs. I'm not yet sure I'll need them, that I'll look at them again before I finish. Meanwhile, all I have to do is run my finger (always with the same amazement) along the eyebrows, the slope of the nose, the fold of the lips, to press the muscle of the tongue to the caves of the cheeks, the bones of the palate. Curved soft clay. A piece of clay You created and You will take.

Oh, the consuming longing to break through. To run right to the end of the thread. To break off all at once. To sink even now into devotion of body and soul. To be concealed in Your arms, even now. Such pleasure…

times on Friday evening, Mother and I would dance a *Krakowiak* on the big rug in the living room. And there was Mother's compulsive forced-labor house cleaning, and her periods of rage and despair when I didn't straighten up my room (what I called "prophecies of rage" with self-defensive cunning), there was the everlasting, frightened struggle to make me eat, and there was the disconnected silence that enveloped her when she didn't get out of bed on Yom Kippur. And there was the photo album "from there" at the bottom of Mother's lingerie drawer, with unfamiliar images, and also pictures of a boy, Marek. And stories about him, joyful, a baby in a cradle on the balcony, a beautiful child on the boulevard. And a tender memory of the goggle-moggle with sugar he loved so much (and only years later did I understand the terrifying circumstances of that). And there were the weekly get-togethers at Aunt Tonka's house (who was never introduced as the widow of Mother's older brother who was murdered), get-togethers so different from the humorous, confident gatherings of Father's family (members of the Third Aliyah and the leadership of the Yishuv and the state). At night, in Aunt Tonka's modest apartment, I was the only little girl—"a blonde, she looks like a *shiksa*"—in the middle of the Polish conversation of "friends from there." And every year there were also the visits of Schindler, when you could go all dressed up with Mother's cousin to greet him at the Dan Hotel. And once, when Mother and I were coming back from the city on bus Number 22, Mother stopped next to the driver and blurted a short sentence at him for no reason. The driver, a gray man in a jacket, was silent and turned his head away. "He was a ca–po," she said when we got off, pronouncing the pair of incomprehensible syllables gravely. All that was part of the cloud that darkened the horizon, yes, but had nothing to do with what was mentioned at school or on the radio.

Poland and Kraków weren't "real" places either, no more than King Solomon's Temple, for instance. I remember how stunned I was when I went with Mother to the film *King Matthew the First*, based on the children's story by Janusz Korzak which I had read in

(And thoughts of little faith, of great anger, embroil my limbs. If only You would call me at once, and not ask me for repentance! If only and at once You would enfold me in Your garb and want me.)…

MICHAL GOVRIN

3
MICHAL GOVRIN,
THE NAME
(NEW YORK
RIVERHEAD
BOOKS, 1998),
3–5.

And may it be Your will to accept me with love and desire. And may it be Your will to answer my plea. And may it be Your will that my little bit of fat and blood be like fat placed on the altar before You.
*And may You want me.*3

The Hebrew root for "pray" [פלל/*peh lamed lamed*] has three meanings. One is to wait, to aspire, to foresee, to hope, or to presume. The second one is to plead, to request. The third one: to judge and to sentence. Three different landscapes of the same root. For the short time we have, I would like to stress the first meaning–of the expectation, the hope, the presumption. Do we ever think about how close prayer and prophecy are as the Hebrew common root reveals? Both of them project a future, and bring it by through the power of language, the power of performance. Both bring, or believe to bring a projected future into reality by the mere power of saying it, as a curse, as a wish, as a blessing, as an oath. Like magic. Yet the most intense expectation of the prayer is for the listener—an expectation and an outrageous confidence —of being listened to. Without the addressing there wouldn't be a prayer. Even wordless, before the first word, the prayer is already addressing. The prayer itself has the power to establish the space of address–to create, to open it. And in a way it does not only create an "I" who has the power to address, but also the addressee.

Although it sounds heretical, it's a very central, traditional Jewish attitude that prayer does create the listening God in the moment of saying the name of "God" in the prayer. At that moment the language induces the listening of God. Yet this indispensable listening is never taken for granted. The listener can always close his ear and turn away. He, or she, needs to be incessantly

Hebrew. In the film, the children spoke Polish! And it didn't sound like the language of the friends at Aunt Tonka's house. "Nice Polish," Mother explained, "of Poles." Poles? They apparently do exist somewhere.

Yet, a few events did form a first bridge between outside and inside. One day, in a used book store in south Tel Aviv, Mother bought an album of black and white photos of Kraków. "Because the photos are beautiful," she emphasized, "they have artistic value." And indeed, the sights of the Renaissance city in the four seasons flowed before my eyes. A beautiful, tranquil city, full of greenery and towers. Jews? No, there were no Jews in that album, maybe only a few alleys "on the way to Kazimierz."

At the age of ten, my parents sent me for private lessons in English, because "it's important to know languages." And thus I came to Mrs. Spiro, a gentle woman from London, married to Doctor Spiro, Mother's classmate from the Hebrew high school in Kraków. One day, when the lesson was over, Mrs. Spiro accompanied me to the edge of the yard of their house on King Solomon Street. I recall the sidewalk with big paving stones as she talked with me. Maybe I had complained before about Mother's strict demands, or maybe she started talking on her own.

"Of course, you know what your mother went through; she was in the Holocaust. You have to understand her, the tensions she has sometimes," she said to me directly.

That was an earthquake. A double one. The understanding that Mother was in "the Holocaust," that awful thing they talk about in school assemblies, with "the six million." And that I, a ten-year-old girl, had to or even could "understand" Mother. That is, to leave the symbiosis of mother and daughter constituting one expanded body, to cut myself off from my child's view, and see Mother as a separate person, with her own fate and reasons for moods that didn't depend only on me, or on my certain guilt. I remember how, at that moment, facing the spotted paving stones, I understood both those things all at once. Like a blinding blow.

seduced to stay longer, to listen some more. Prayer is thus an act of seduction, a cry of desire of the beloved to the lover to be accepted. As Amalia says in a quote from the Jewish prayer, "and may You accept me." That's what every language and address says, *May you accept me.* And the prayer is usually short, a Psalm can be two, three, five minutes long. It does not have the narrative breath of a whole Arabian Night, its rhetorical devices of seduction intensely shift from praise to imploring, from self-submission to chanting, from despair to celebrating. An intensity that betrays the fragility of the address, the awareness that the listener can disappear any moment, and with it the possibility to pray. And how close prayer is to writing: sitting in the loneliness of your room and addressing, believing that this address will once be read, be received and using all the rhetorical devices to seduce that listener, the reader, to stay there. And how erotically charged the prayer is. When Amalia prays "and may You accept me", by the simple fact that the prayer is literally said by a woman—and the naked literal is always the most powerful—her prayer becomes an audacious erotic act, and a gesture of transgression. The Jewish prayers were composed by men and were seen as said mainly by men. Their overt erotic dimension was immediately reduced to a metaphor for the relationship between the nation, the bride, and God, the groom. To pray through fiction and through the lips of a woman became a gesture of transgression. I rediscovered, to my amazement, the common place fact that there is not a single book in the whole Jewish tradition—liturgical, halachic, mystical—signed by a woman. None of the books that entered the canon was ever attributed to a woman. There are female characters, but they never have an independent voice. So, the feeling of transgression at the moment of writing was a confirmation that something alive was occurring, some concealed electricity was coming through.

MICHAL GOVRIN

Then came high school in Tel Aviv. Since both the principal and the assistant principal were graduates of the Hebrew High School in Kraków, their former classmates in that high school, including my mother, sent their children to study there. At that school, influenced by the principal and his assistant, both of them historians, there was an intense awareness of the Jewish past and life in the Diaspora—a rare dimension in the Zionist Israeli landscape of Diaspora denial—and Gideon Hausner, the prosecutor in the Eichmann Trial, initiated a "club to immortalize the Jewish community of Kraków." A group of students met with members of the Kraków community, who taught them the history of the city and the Jewish community before the destruction. The club also heard testimony from the Holocaust, with a special (exclusive?) emphasis on the activities of the Jewish underground. The women's revolt in the Gestapo prison, led by Justina, was also dramatized and performed for the community on the annual memorial day. (Holocaust "celebrations," as they were called by members of the drama club.)

I was a member of the "club to immortalize," and I also played a Polish cook in the performance of the history of the uprising. But in fact, a partition still remained between me and the others, a zone of silence so dense that, to this day, I don't know which of the children of the Kraków community members were children of Holocaust survivors and not of parents who emigrated to Palestine before the war. If there were any, no bond was formed between us. We didn't talk about it. We remained isolated, caged in the sealed biographies of our parents.

There were other bridges here too, almost subterranean ones, which, as far as I recall, were not formulated explicitly. The bond with the literature teacher, the poet, Itamar Yaoz-Kest, who survived as a child with his mother in Bergen-Belsen. In high school, there were only his influence on my literary development and a sense of closeness, a sort of secret look between "others." (Only later did I read the poems of *The Double Root* about his childhood "there," and his story describing, as he put it, a little girl who looked

MICHAL GOVRIN

To go from language to the body, I think that one of my *teachers* in understanding Jewish prayer was, with no doubt, Antonin Artaud. *His* definition of performed language as "hieroglyphs in the body," led me to understand the prayer as an extreme mode of being a sign, where the body, the gestures, the voice, the silence are all inscribed signs. As said in Psalms, 35:10: All my bones shall speak. Or in Job, "out of my flesh I shall see God." And the context in Job offers a striking anatomy of prayer as inscription.

Oh, that my words were recorded, that they were inscribed in the book! Oh, that with an iron pen they were engraved on a rock and sealed with lead for ever! For I know that my Redeemer lives, and at last he will stand upon the earth;…and after [under] my skin has thus been destroyed [engraved], then, out of my flesh I shall see God. 4

Once the words of the prayers are marked into the body, in the singular seal of soul and flesh, inscribed on the tablet of the heart, on the parchment of the skin, only at that moment one can see God. One sees the god that has been inscribed in the flesh. One sees with the eyes of the flesh.

But what if the engraved prayer bursting out from behind the skin is a buried shout?

Tractate Berachot, regulating Jewish prayer, was compiled right after the destruction of the second Temple in Jerusalem by the Romans, and this trauma shadows its entirety. Other significant parts of the liturgy, mainly those of the High Holidays, echo the massacres during the crusades. Jewish prayer bursts out at the shadow of destruction and persecution, from places of ruins. Rejoice with trembling5 is the talmudic definition of a state of mind of someone who prays and remembers.6 A dimension still almost absent from the prayer after the Holocaust, either postponed by the urgency to rebuild the devastated communities and to

4
JOB 19:23–26
I ADD IN BRACKETS ANOTHER POSSIBILITY OF TRANSLATION.

5
PSALMS 2:11

6
TALMUD, BERACHOT, 30B

like me, the daughter of survivors.) And there was the love affair with the boy in my class, whose delicate smile on his drooping lower lip looked like the "different" smile of the literature teacher. His father, the lawyer, submitted reparations claims to Germany in those days–close enough to the seductive-dangerous realm. My complicated relations with that boy paralleled the shock of my discovery of Kafka; and along with the tempest of feelings of fifteen -year-olds, that forbidden, denied, inflamed relation also had a pungent mixture of eros and sadism, a tenderness and an attraction to death, and above all, metaphysical dimensions that pierced the abyss of dark feelings which somehow was also part of "there."

In my childhood, Mother was an omnipotent entity within the house, I couldn't "understand" her. Later, when she became the authority to rebel against, the enzyme necessary to cut the fruit off from the branch erected a dam of alienation and enmity between us; I couldn't identify with her, with her humanity. There had to be a real separation. I had to live by myself. To go through the trials alone. To listen slowly to what was concealed.

An amazing example of the layers of memory and forgetting was revealed to me as I wrote *The Name*. The only detail I borrowed in the novel from things I had heard from Mother was a story of the heroism of a woman who succeeded in escaping from Auschwitz-Birkenau, and when she was caught and taken to the *Appelplatz*, she managed to commit suicide. I also borrowed the admiring tone in which Mother spoke of the event. (Only later did I discover how it had served her as a model.) I created a biographical-fictional character, a virtuoso pianist, and invented a name for her—Mala—immortalized in the name of the heroine, Amalia. Years later, as I was finishing the book, I came across a written description of the event in Birkenau and discovered that the name of the woman was the same name I had "invented," "Mala"–Mala Zimetbaum.

Then came the move to Europe, to Paris. To study for the doctorate and to write literature intensively. I went to the Paris of

claim a new State, or eclipsed by the celebratory oblivious-
ness of western Jewish renewal, alien to the responsibility
to remember...above my chief joy. 7

MICHAL GOVRIN

After the destruction of the Temple in Jerusalem,
personal and communal prayer become a substitute to
the Temple ritual, and the designated central meeting
place between God and the People is disseminated to
any synagogue and to any place where a Jew prays.
There is an urgency in Berachot to build a body of prayer,
yet, throughout the tractate there is a prevailing sense
of fragility, of fear, of doubt lest the divorce was irreme-
diable, lest the link between God and the People was
irrevocably interrupted. In one of the somberist moments
of the Tractate Rabbi Elazar states: from the day the Temple
was destroyed the Gates of Prayer were locked,8 as it was said:
Even when I cry aloud and call for help, He shuts out my prayer. 9
In Lamentations, written after the destruction of the
first Temple, God himself is imprisoned by His own rage
and is unwilling to listen.

> We have transgressed and rebelled, and Thou hast not
> forgiven. Thou hast clothed Thyself with anger and pur-
> sued us; Thou hast slain and hast not pitied. Thou hast
> screened Thyself with a cloud through which our wor
> ship cannot pass. 10

Still, Rabbi Elazar leaves an open window: Even if the
Gates of Prayer were locked, nevertheless the Gates of Tears
were not locked. 11 As is said, Hear my prayer, O Lord, and give
ear unto thy cry; hold not thy peace [deafness] at my tears. 12

We find here the tear—the physical embodiment of
emotion, of pain—a theme that Jacques Derrida has
treated many times so beautifully. There is nothing,
according to the Talmud, that will not melt by the tear's
outpour, by its power to radically change even the most
sealed situation, even God's wrath. The tear is the last
resource of the most hurt, the most fragile, whose cry
pours out, irresistibly, like tears; the desperate weapon

7
PSALMS 137:6

8
TALMUD,
BREACHOT, 32B

9
LAMENTATIONS
3:8

10
LAMENTATIONS
3:42–44

OVER THE YEARS
THE BOOK OF
LAMENTATIONS
BECAME FOR ME
ONE OF THE
MOST UNIVERSAL
CRIES AGAINST
THE ATROCITIES
OF WAR. AN
ACUTE ACCOUNT
OF THE BESIEGED
DISTRESS, ALWAYS
IGNORED BY
THOSE OUTSIDE
THE WALLS,
UNLISTENED TO
BY EITHER
"HUMAN" OR
"DIVINE" EARS.
THIS INCAPACITY
TO HEAR THE
AFFLICTED IS THE
MADNESS IN THE
CORE OF ALL
WARS; THE
FORGETFULNESS,
ESPECIALLY, OF
HOW MUCH
THIS SITUATION
IS REVERSIBLE,
AND THAT YOU,
THE POWERFUL
OF TODAY, WILL
TOMORROW
FIND YOURSELF
INSIDE THE WALLS
OF HORROR, AND
YOUR CRIES WILL
REMAIN
UNLISTENED.

11
IBID.

12
PSALMS 39:13

culture, of Rilke, of Proust, of Edith Piaf. But in 1972, soon after I arrived, the film *The Sorrow and the Pity* by Marcel Ophuls was released. When the screening ended in the cinema on the Champs-Élysées, I emerged into a different Paris, into a place where that mythical war had gone. I "understood" that here, on Rue de Rivoli, beneath my garret room, German tanks had passed (ever since then they began to inhabit my dreams); I "understood" that the description of the French as a nation of bold underground fighters and rescuers of Jews—a notion I had grown up with in the years of the military pact between Israel and de Gaulle's France—was very far from reality. The clear, comforting borders between good and bad were shattered for me, and so were the simple moral judgements mobilized for ideologies. Here, far from a post-Six-Day War Israel secure in her power, far from the official versions of Holocaust and heroism, a different time was in the streets, a time not completely cut off from the war years. Here, for the fist time I experienced the sense of the *other*. As a Jew, as an Israeli. Wary of revealing my identity at the university that served as a center of *Fatah* activities, trembling in the *Métro* once as I read the Israeli newspaper, *Ma'ariv*, until someone called it to my attention: "*Mademoiselle*, somebody spat on your jacket."

Distance also allowed a different discourse with my parents, especially with Mother. In the weekly letters, without the daily tension of life at home, a new bond was formed, between people who were close, who were beginning to speak more openly with one another. Even my clothes in European winter, in the "retro" style, began to look like the clothes in Mother's old pictures from Poland, like her hairdo in the photo next to the jeep from Hanover, when she served after the war as a commander in Aliyah B, the *Brikha*, camouflaged in an UNRRA uniform. Poland, Hanover, suddenly turned into places that were much closer, more present than the little state on the shores of the Mediterranean.

On the first Holocaust Memorial Day in Paris, I decided to stay in my apartment all day and to cut myself off from the street

of the most silenced, who are often compared to women. And thus, in a striking way, the rabbis in Berachot learn how to pray from a woman: Hannah, a barren woman whose distress is buried and whose womb is mute. From this total concealment her prayer and tears burst out:

MICHAL GOVRIN

> And she was in bitterness of soul, and prayed unto the Lord, and wept sore. [13]

13
SAMUEL I 1:10

14
SAMUEL I 2:1

The distressed shout bursting out from a woman's womb, like the blowing of the Shofar compared to the shouts of the birth giving woman, is for the Talmud the exemplary prayer, one that can shatter God who is blamed as the cause of her childlessness. It is God's own barrenness that her desperate prayer aims to shatter, and her tears to melt, with an oath—another mode of prophetic-magic prayer. A prayer that has the power to shake God out of his concealment and refusal to listen. Only then, much later, when desire and fertility are restored with the birth giving to Samuel, joy flows forth:

> My heart rejoices in the Lord, mine horn is exalted in the Lord: my mouth is enlarged over mine enemies; because I rejoice in my salvation. [14]

Hannah's distressed prayer of a barren woman is described physically, moving her lips, shaking her whole body. And I thought to myself that what could have been easily called "female madness" or "hysteria" (bursting from the uterus: *ustera*) becomes here the essential prayer. The Talmud amplifies the biblical irony at Eli who watches Hannah with an external gaze totally blind to what he sees.

> As she continued praying before the Lord, Eli noticed her mouth, for Hannah was speaking in her heart; her lips moved, but no voice could be heard so that Eli thought that she was drunk.

that lived by its own dates (for example, Armistice Day of World War I, the "Great War" that took place at the same time of the year). I spent the day reading works on the sources of Nazism, on the roots of anti-Semitism, on the German nationalism of Wagner (rehearsals of whose *Parsifal* I had attended at the Paris Opera).

That summer, on a tour of Europe, an accident forced me to stay unexpectedly in Munich for three weeks. And then the blank spot that filled the heart of the European map for me— Germany—the blank, untouchable spot that sucked up all the evil, also fell. Here, next to the beer hall of "the Nazi buds," where some Israelis had taken me, in what was obviously a sick gesture, there was also an opera, where Mozart was performed, and there were wonderful museums and parks.

The forced stay in Germany and the Yom Kippur War the following autumn, which I spent in Paris facing the brightly lit Champs-Élysées while my dear ones were in mortal danger, proved to me that there is no refuge in the soothing distinctions between "then" and "now," between "there" and "here." And I also understood that there is no racial difference, imprinted at birth between "them" and "us," nor can we hide behind the fences of the Chosen People. And that, in every person, the murderer and the victim potentially exist, blended into one another, constantly demanding separation, every single day, with full awareness. I understood that I could no longer hide behind the collective, ready-made definitions of memory. That there would be no choice but to embark on the journey that is obstinate, lonely, and full of contradictions.

Germany, France, Europe. What is in that culture, in its roots, mixed with the gold of the baroque and the flickering brasses of symphonies; what is in the squares, in the churches, in the ideologies that allowed what happened? Prepared it? Didn't prevent it? What inflamed the hatred? What repressed it under pious words of morality? What fostered it in the heart of religious belief? What prepared it in the tales of God that man told himself to justify the outbursts of his evil instincts under the disguise of *Imitatio Dei*?

So Eli said to her, How long will you behave as one intoxicated? Get rid of your wine.

But Hannah replied, No, my master, I am a deeply grieved woman, I have drunk no wine or liquor, but I have poured out my soul before the Lord. Do not consider your maid a good-for-nothing; for I have spoken all the while under stress of provocation and distress.[15]

You can never understand a prayer from the outside, you have to be inside in order to understand it.[16]

The Talmud compares the prayer of Hannah to those of Elija or Moses, who, by their prayer, force God to change his mind and give up his plan to destroy the sinful people. This extreme shout which is on the edge of blasphemy is called "to fling" or "to hurl words towards Heaven." [הטיח/ה דברים כלפי מעלה/*heticha* or *hetiach devarim klapei mala*.[17]] It's difficult to find the translation. In Hebrew it means to shout or to literally throw words at heaven, in a very extreme and non-referential way. And this is, for the talmudic rabbis, the model of prayer after the destruction, a prayer that takes on itself the extreme task of shaking God from his paralysis and rage, of shaking the world out of the mechanism of destruction.

This image of an impotent, helpless God has many versions. In the Midrash there's a description of Rachel arguing with God after the destruction of Jerusalem, accusing God of having abandoned His children and herself. She does not accept any of His answers. She is not comforted. Later, in the parallel passage of the Zohar, Rachel is even more extreme. The traditional understanding of Rachel's lament, as it figures in Jeremiah[18], is that she weeps over the death of her children. In the Zohar, there is an audacious shift of understanding. Towards the end of Rachel's lamentation in Jeremiah, the language shifts from the plural to the singular in an irregular way. The text says, Rachel,

MICHAL GOVRIN

15
SAMUEL I 1:12–16

16
THE FOUNDER OF HASIDISM, RABBI ISRAEL BA'AL SHEM TOV MADE A COMPARISON: HE IS PRAYING LIKE SOMEONE WHO IS DROWNING IN A RIVER, AND STRUGGLING TO SAVE HIS LIFE. SOMEONE WHO CROSSES THE BRIDGE AND SEES HIM DOWN THERE IS WONDERING, WHY DOES HE GESTICULATE IN SUCH A STRANGE MANNER?

17
TALMUD, BERACHOT, 31B

18
JEREMIAH 31:14–20

And what still exists right before my eyes? Keeps on happening?

How to draw the borders between good and bad with a thin scalpel under a microscope? How to distinguish anew, here and now? All the time?

And what is the terrorizing persuasive force of tales and their metamorphoses into theologies, ideologies? How to struggle with forgetting, with denial, without whitewashing, but also without reiterating the same stories, without inflaming the same evil instincts? How to tell responsibly?

Jarring questions that filled me, that nourished my research, my theatrical productions, my literary writing, but did not yet touch Mother's hidden place.

I spent the summer of 1975 between Princeton and New York, collecting material for my doctorate, reading the works of Rabbi Nahman of Bratzlav in the JTS library, and in the evenings, swallowing the plethora of fringe theater, jazz, and transvestite clubs, and the international bohemian life of Manhattan. And thus I met that young violinist from Kraków who had fled Poland, and was working as a cabdriver. A handsome young man from Kraków. Kraków? A place where people live?! The summer romance was a way to confront the profound seduction of the depths of the past stamped in me, as well as the depths of my femininity.

One day that summer, my aunt, Mother's sister-in-law, came to my apartment in midtown Manhattan. I vaguely knew her from a visit she had made to Israel years before, and after the death of Aunt Tonka in Tel Aviv, my aunt from Queens, the widow of Mother's second brother, who perished in the camps, was her last living close relative. She had survived Aushwitz and her young son was hidden by a Christian woman. After the war, my aunt and her son emigrated to New York.

That day, on the balcony on the thirtieth floor, facing the roofs of midtown Manhattan, my aunt spoke in broken English only about "then" and "there," as if here and now didn't exist, as

weeping for her children, refuses to be comforted for her children, because He is not.[19] The Zohar uses this irregularity to suggest a subversive understanding.[20] Accordingly, Rachel does not only lament the death of her children, but the absence of God—because *He is not* [כי איננו/*ki einenu*]. As if by the extremity of His rage and punishment, He mutilated Himself and disappeared, to the point that "He is not". Rachel's tears and uncomforted lament succeed, in the Zohar, to shatter God, make him regret his rage and return to Rachel and his People.[21]

I was very moved to find, while writing *The Name*, the notes of Rabbi Klonimus of Piasechna, a young Hasidic master, who went on teaching in the Warsaw ghetto until he was sent to the Death Camp. His extraordinary manuscript was buried in a milk tank. It was found in the 1950s, under the rubble of the former ghetto, and published as *Holy Fire*.[22] He quotes the Talmud and the Zohar to be able to claim belief in the face of the destruction. His voice was almost not followed after the Holocaust. Only in the ghetto was there courage to say that God was so consumed by rage that He was helpless. In the Rabbi of Piasechna's *Holy Fire*, there is a total reversal of roles: man takes responsibility for God. It's a form of resistance. We cannot wait passively. We have to take the first step. We will weep, with the power of our tears, we can help God shed tears with us, and by this shared lament free God—and with him, humankind—from the rage of destruction. A kind of taking over...with a prayer.

To finish, I'll offer you—before going to the very last words of Amalia's prayer—a text which was before me the whole time that I was writing. There are two quotes in the Talmud, in Menahot 29B and in Berachot 68B describing, in the elliptic Talmudic style, the life and death in prayer of Rabbi Akiba ben Joseph, one of the main masters of the Mishna, who lived in the 1st and 2nd century A.D. As I followed the evolving stages

MICHAL GOVRIN

19
JEREMIAH 31:15

20
ZOHAR,
LAMENTATIONS,
92B

21
FOR MORE
ABOUT GOD'S
FLAW IN EARLY
KABBALAH SEE: H.
PEDAYA, FLAW
AND CORRECTION
IN THE CONCEPT
OF THE GODHEAD
IN THE TEACHING
OF RABBI ISSAC
THE BLIND,
JSJT, 6, 1987.

22
RABBI KLONIMUS
OF PIASECHNA,
HOLY FIRE,
JERUSALEM, 1960.

if we had never left there. She and the Polish pop music at night melted the last wall of resistance. Now I had no excuse not to translate my preoccupation with the subject into action, no excuse not to go to Poland.

In late October, after the administrative alibi was concocted in Paris, I left. Ready. And not ready at all.

I was not ready for what I would find or for what I would not. I was not ready for the fear. The fear of returning to the strange hotel room at night, the primal fear that I would starve to death, which impelled me to eat nonstop, completely violating the rules of *Kashrut* which I had observed ever since I came to Paris to study, eating with the dispensation "allowed during an emergency," that I granted myself (insolently?). Not ready for the fear that rushed me in a panic straight from the visit to Auschwitz-Birkenau to meetings with Polish artists and to bohemian parties. I was especially not ready for the complexity of my responses, for their force. For what was revealed to me in "the living laboratory" I had poured by myself. The contradictory burst of fascination and revulsion, alienation and belonging, shame and vengeance, of helplessness, of complete denial....

When I returned, the letter to my parents was a first attempt to look at what was revealed, to talk. The restrained language of the letter reflects the difficulty of going beyond the taboo, hoping they would understand through the silence. That different, new discourse with my parents accompanied us throughout the years until their death. A discourse of closeness, of belonging, of acceptance, beyond the generational differences.

The sense of belonging—along with my parents—to the "other, Jewish story" revealed in the depths of the journey only intensified in the following years, as the doors to the centers of European culture opened to me, as I devoted myself to writing. But at the same time, the understanding that it is impossible to go on telling as if nothing had happened also grew. The understanding that, after Auschwitz, there were no more stories that did not betray, there were no more innocent stories.

of mind of my character, I kept reading these quotes in different ways; they always changed, amazingly, like a kaleidoscope; and still now I am not sure what is the meaning of Rabbi Akiva's last lesson (very much like Socrates) at the moment of his execution by the Romans. I give them to you as an open-ended text, for you to go on thinking about. Just few words about the Talmudic context of the second part, in which the meaning of the prayer, *Sh'ma Ysra'el* (Hear O Israel) is debated. The origin of this fundamental Jewish prayer is in Deuteronomy:

> Hear O Israel, the Lord is God, the Lord is One.
> And you shall love the Lord your God with all your heart, with all your soul, and with all your strength. 23

Actually Rabbi Akiba's death is an existential commentary of the expression "you shall love the Lord your God, with all your soul." The last teaching of Akiba, taught through prayer, with his own flesh and soul, beyond words. When words and body are one.

> Rab Judah said in the name of Rab, When Moses ascended on high he found the Holy One, blessed be He, engaged in affixing coronets to the letters. Said Moses: Lord of the Universe, who stays Thy hand?
>
> He answered: There will arise a man, at the end of many generations, Akiba ben Joseph by name, who will expound upon each tittle heaps and heaps of laws.
>
> Lord of the Universe, said Moses, permit me to see him.
>
> He replied, Turn thee around.
>
> Moses went and sat down behind eight rows. 24
>
> Not being able to follow their arguments he was ill at ease, but when they came to a certain subject and the disciples said to the master [to Rabbi Akiba]: Whence do you know it? and the latter replied: It is a law given unto Moses at Sinai, he was comforted.
>
> Thereupon he returned to the Holy One, blessed be He, and said: Lord of the Universe, Thou hast such a man and Thou givest the Torah by me!

MICHAL GOVRIN

23
DEUTERONOMY
6:4–5

24
WHICH MEANS AT
THE BACK ROW
OF RABBI AKIBA'S
SCHOOL.

And what about Mother's shrouded "story"? Details continued to join together in fragments. For years, here and there, she mentioned events, some in conversations with me, some in conversations with others which I chanced upon. I listened when she spoke, and she spoke little. Never did I "interview" her; never did I ask. I respected her way of speaking, as well as her way of being silent. Even after I returned from Auschwitz, I didn't think she had to report or that I had to (or could) "know." I learned from her lesson of telling in silence.

I heard the first fragment of a chronological description from my mother under extraordinary circumstances. In the autumn of 1977, she was summoned to give testimony in a German court in Hanover. I accompanied my parents to the trial, sitting with Father in the gallery and seeing Mother, with her special erect posture, surrounded by the black robes of the attorneys. In her fluent German, she described the Plaszów camp, where Jews from the Kraków Ghetto were removed; she pointed authoritatively at the maps. Her voice trembled only a moment when she came to description of the *Kinderheim*, the children's home in Plaszów, where children were taken from their parents. In a few words, she dealt with the *Aktsia*, told how all the inmates of the camp were taken out to the square while an orchestra played lullabies, to see how the SS loaded the children onto the trucks that took them to the gas chambers. She was asked what was the name of her son, and how old he was at the time of the *Aktsia*. She replied with and effort, "Marek. Eight years old." The prosecutor asked for a momentary recess, and then the questions resumed. (That prosecutor accompanied us when we left, apologizing in shame for the accused, the deputy of Emon Gantt, the commander of Plaszów, who was absent from the courtroom "for medical reasons.")

A few years later, Mother tried to dramatize the story of the revolt of the women in Kraków at the vocational high school where she taught, wanting to bring the subject close to her women students. She worked with Father on the script and developed original

He replied, Silence,[25] for such is My decree.

Then said Moses: Lord of the Universe, Thou hast shown me his Torah, show me his reward.

Turn thee around, said He; and Moses turned around and saw them weighing out his flesh at the market stalls. Lord of the Universe, cried Moses, such Torah, and such a reward!

He replied, Silence [Shut up], for such is My decree.

When Rabbi Akiba was taken out for execution, it was the hour for the recital of the Sh'ma, and while they flayed his flesh with iron combs, he was accepting upon himself the kingship of heaven. His disciples said to him, Our teacher, even to this point? He said to them, All my days I have been troubled by this verse, *with all my soul*—even if He takes my soul. I said, When shall I have the opportunity of fulfilling this? Now that I have the opportunity shall I not fulfill it? He prolonged the word Ehad—One—until he expired while saying it.[26]

MICHAL GOVRIN

25
AND THE ACTUAL TRANSLATION PERHAPS SHOULD BE SHUT UP AND NOT SILENCE.

26
GOVRIN THE NAME, 359–60. AMALIA, THE NARRATOR, IS QUOTING HERE FROM THE TALMUD: MENACHOT, 29B AND BERACHOT, 68B.

To write through a prayer was an urge for me. To Amalia's final prayer, at the end of *The Name*, I was also led by an urge, from within, from inside the space. At a certain moment an uncontrollable—and at the time incomprehensible—urge pushed me to break Amalia's prayer. A mighty resistance against her desire to become God's bride, full of the *hubris* of being the "only one," the "chosen" (the core of monotheistic fanaticism), and without remembering that the "I" you utter in the prayer can be uttered by so many others. But mainly I was pushed to break her self-accusation, taking on herself an almost Christian role to expiate suffering by sacrificing herself, by taking God's, the world's sufferings on her. Was I voicing my mother's silent, buried shout, her unsettled trial against God? Amalia's ecstatic submission and prayer became for me imprisoning, bare and unbearable hypocrisy in the wake of destruction. I could not contain myself, I had to push her to hurl words against heaven, to blaspheme. The freeing of another prayer within Amalia's prayer had to pass

ideas of staging designed to increase audience participation. But, during the rehearsals, she developed such a serious skin disease, clearly as a reaction, that the doctor advised her to stop the production.

The presence of the Holocaust receded completely in her last months, as she struggled with the fatal cancer that was discovered in her. Death was too close to think about its old dread–at any rate, that was my feeling as I stood at her side, admiring her yearning for life, the audacity, the amazing black humor, which restored the dimensions of human absurdity even in the most difficult situations. The day before she lost consciousness, she spoke a lot, in a stupor, in Polish. What did she say? Was she still living there? I couldn't go with her. I remained alone, at her bedside. Then, as I was massaging her feet, those feet that had marched in the death march through frozen Europe, I was struck with the simple knowledge that it was to Mother's struggle, there, that I owed my birth.

I heard Mother's "story" only after her death–death that always turns a loved one into a "story" with a beginning and an end. During the *Shiva*, Rivka Horowitz came to Jerusalem from Bnei-Brak. A woman with bold blue eyes, whom I knew only by name. She was one of nine women, all of them graduates of Beit Yaov, the ultra-orthodox school for girls in Kraków, whom my mother joined in the ghetto, despite differences of education and ideology. The ten women, "The *Minyan*," supported one another in the ghetto, during the years in the Plaszów camp, in Auschwitz-Birkenau, throughout the death march, and in the final weeks in Bergen-Belsen. For two years, they hadn't abandoned one another; together they fought exhaustion and disease, lived through the selections, until all of them survived. "There was strength in them. Moral strength," Mother explained when she and Father, both of them members of the liberal, secular *Mapai*, assiduously attended the celebrations of the friends in Bnei-Brak. At the *Shiva*, I heard from Rivka Horowitz for the first time about that period.

through breaking. And only then, frightened by this urge, I discovered that it is impossible to really blaspheme, to break the space of address by blasphemy. God ("this bastard" as Beckett said), stays the indispensable addressee even at the extremity of blasphemy, that might be one of the strongest forms of address, of prayer.

MICHAL GOVRIN

When Amalia finishes her prayer at the end of the book she is already in another stage, turning towards Sabbath. While writing those pages I thought about the end of another prayer of life–that of Paul Celan, and the last word of his last, postume poem, *"Rebleute graben"*: *"am Sabbath"*.[27]

27
IN PAUL CELAN:
ZEITGEHÖFT,
1976.

And in a way, my architecture, and Amalia's, at the end, is of breaking: from the crescendo of the forty-nine days of the Counting of the Omer towards the Sabbath, the day of weekly rest; from a desire for cleavage, for self-submission, to a gesture of release, of acceptance... of just opening. And I'll read Amalia's last words:

> The body is silent, wrapped in a distant dizziness. Like standing on the edge of a cliff. The paper and the fingers guiding the pen are slipping away. And now I don't know anymore if the Sabbath has started. The border is blurred. A whiteness is spreading now like a deep sleep behind the eyes. What a great blessing.
>
> The time has come. Just to go on turning now, with no expectations anymore, for an answer.... Just to go on turning to what is gaping there in the calm. Everything I shall give You. Everything. *Enter, O Bride.*
>
> Just to go on turning, that's the prayer. Just to go on turning in the expanding space.
>
> And the voice speaking between us is enough. Enough the words of the prayer muttered from my lips.
>
> For that the blessing, *My Lord, open my lips.* For that. Just open more. You'll just go on muttering the voice from my throat, my tongue, my lips. Without any expectation anymore that You will accept, that You will hear.
>
> And maybe that is the answer. Finally. That is the answer.

She spoke for a few hours—out of a responsibility to tell me—and left. And after that, we didn't meet again. Later on, when I was almost finished writing *The Name* (and after Mother's death, it seemed to me that, more than ever, the novel spoke of a "there" that was lost forever), came the first information about the family property in Kraków. Apartment houses, a button factory.... Property? There? "In the regions of delusion?" And then, the name that had been common at home, Schindler, which suddenly became a book and then a film, and turned into a general legacy the story of the rescue of Mother's cousin and his wife, Mother's refusal to join the list of workers in the enamel factory in order to stay with Marek.

And then, one evening, the telephone rings in Jerusalem, and on the other end of the line, in English with a thick Polish accent, another member of that "*Minyan*" introduces herself, Pearl Benisch, who published a book in 1991, *To Vanquish the Dragon*, with the full story of the group (from the author's religious perspective). A copy arrived on Friday. On the Sabbath eve, I sat with my two little daughters in the living room and picked up the book. I leafed through it distractedly, until I came to the description of the destruction of the *Kinderheim*. And then I fled to the other room so the children wouldn't see me, and there I burst into sobs I didn't know they were hidden inside me. A weeping that arose from there. Mine? Hers?

Until dawn that Sabbath, I read for the first time the story of Mother, in chronological order, dated, revealing the few facts I knew situated in their context. Even the description of the goggle-moggle with sugar that she had secretly made for Marek in the sewing workshop, where the women from Plaszów worked, smuggling the treat to the child when she came back. And how one day the Jewish supervisor discovered her stealing the egg and threatened to turn her in. And how she stood before him then in mortal danger, and accused him in front of all the workers of the sewing shop of being a traitor to his people. I read how in the *Aktsia* of the

A calm. Suspended meanwhile, in the realm that is opening, with the exhalation of the breath in the turning.

MICHAL GOVRIN

Some calm in giving myself to what is opened, comes, to what is standing there. Even though I will never know if its appeal will be granted.

And past and present and future are mixed up. Without giving, without taking. For all is one....
The light is fading. I took a long time to light the candles. I nearly crossed, Holy, Awesome, the border of the hour.

Only the relaxation. The rest from all work, without completion, without finishing. That's what the blessing is for. A relaxation of effort. Like lying on the ground, clinging to the warm dirt. In eternal rest. Open. The relaxation of holding. The calm that breaks out of the silent maw of the Sabbath.

To open the relaxation. To open. More. To let go. To forget. To open to the Sabbath flooding now. A taste of the World to Come. The submission to what is rising there, cloaked in darkness like an animal. Everything, everything I shall give to You. In one. *Ehad.*

My God and God of my fathers, *may You be pleased with my rest, may You be pleased with my rest.*

And the voice of the trumpet sounded long and waxed louder and louder. And the evening is quiet, so sweet in the dryness that is opened.

And in the morning, Shavuoth, the fiftieth day, at dawn, when I shall wear white, ready, the swallows will be shaken out of the Wailing Wall. Slicing with their nimble bodies. Plunging. Casting shadows running over the heads of the packed audience, on the seared dust in the first light of sunrise. They will pass dizzily, inscribing quick lines in the stone.

The remnant of the light on the peak opposite is wiped out. Put down the pen.

The Lord gives and the Lord takes away; blessed be the Name of the Lord.

Sabbath. [28]

destruction of the children's home, against the horrifying back-ground of lullabies, Mother burst into the square toward the SS men who were pushing the weeping children onto the trucks. She shouted to them to take her with the child. And how her friends, the women of the *Minyan*, held her with all their might, pulled her back. I read about the sisterhood between the women in the group, about the pride, the unbelievable humor, how with astonishing freedom they managed to maintain their humanity in the *Lagers* of Auschwitz-Birkenau. They and many other women and men were described in their humanity facing the crematoria. How they suc-ceeded in putting on makeup to get through the selections, how they sneaked the weak women out of line of the condemned, how they secretly lit candles at Hanukkah and held a Passover Seder, and how, after the death march from Auschwitz to Bergen-Belsen, they still managed to laugh together when they got the wrong size prison uniforms. I read, frozen stiff, how, in Bergen-Belsen, Mother dared to be insolent to the female SS officer with the pride she still had left, surviving the public whipping, which few survived, with-out shouting, "so as not to give the SS the pleasure." Between the pages, the figure of Mother returned to me, cheering the women in Auschwitz with stories of her visit to the Land of Israel, singing them songs of the homeland on their muddy beds, where they fell exhausted with typhus and teeming with lice, in Bergen-Belsen. Suddenly I understood one of the few stories Mother had told me about the camps, how she would sing to herself Tchernihovsky's poem: "You may laugh, laugh at the dreams, I the dreamer am telling you, I believe in Man, and in his spirit, his powerful spirit," emphasizing with her off-key voice the words: "I believe in Man, and in his spirit, his powerful spirit...."

Mother's "story." Discovering it in the heart of the journey to what was stamped inside me. Discovering it now in the middle of life, when I myself am a mother, and older than she–the young woman and mother who was there.

"Mother's story," or maybe only milestones around what will remain hidden.

Sabbath.
Just from a construction to no construction.
To the open.

I know that in the morning we wake up with a prayer that   DAVID SHAPIRO
is simply thanking. Well, I thank Michal for her presenta-
tion because I know how hard it is to do. And one thing I
wanted to say was that we really hope that you will look
at this book, which I think is so extraordinary, *The Name.* I
want to ask Jacques to speak now if he wants. I also grew
up in a strange house which was largely not observant
except that my grandfather, the Cantor, Berele Chagy was
always singing. I grew up with the sense that the prayer
was a part of music, and I always miss music. One of the
things that I feel, as Paul Schindler once said, was that the
body *has* the voice, the voice is the wandering part of the
body. And so I'd like to ask Jacques whether he'd like to talk
about this. I know that suddenly I have a list of questions
and today, my friend a painter in Los Angeles said, "Don't
ask him questions! He can improvise without it," so, like a
Cantor, I hope you'll improvise on the subject.

I have a question about improvisation. Well, this is the   JACQUES DERRIDA
moment of paralysis that Michal referred to, a moment
of paralysis. I must confess, (that is the topic of the book,
confessing), it's impossible for me to say something
just. Perhaps I should say listen to her, read *The Name*
that's all. A moment of paralysis. And since you mentioned improvisation, I was hesitating between two
ethics of prayer, so to speak. Two definitions of prayer.
One has to do with improvisation. The prayer should
be, in principle, pure improvisation. A way of inventing
on the spot, the address, the addressee, the language,
the code, so there shouldn't be any book, any program,
any rule to pray, on the one hand. Speaking of music, in
that extent, jazz would be closer to prayer.... But we
know that in jazz there are rules too.... So, although we

MICHAL GOVRIN.

LETTER from REGIONS OF DELUSION

November 2, 1975, Paris

My dears,

Back home–what a relief!

A week in Poland is like a year, like years, like a moment. Ever since the visa was approved, a week before the trip, I felt as if I were facing an operation. I was waiting for something to stop me, for an iron curtain to block the way. And even in the dark, when the bus took us from the plane to the airport in Warsaw, I still didn't believe that the distance between me and Poland would be swallowed up just like that, in a few steps.

Your letter, which reached me just before the trip, was a lifeline in moments when the dizziness intensified; in moments when there was only a definite absence of my imaginary picture of those places, when instead, there were only the long lines in gray rain-coats; in moments of awful loneliness, when there was no one to shout at; in moments when I didn't believe I could finally get on the train and leave that madness behind.

How to tell, and wasn't there any chronology? How to live that over again?

Wroclaw. A dreary city and a theater festival. I was ejected into the darkness in the heart of an empty field. That's how it began. Night in the hotel. An enormous radio, and voices from Russian, Polish, Czech, and Hungarian stations. Stifling heat from the fur-nace, the chambermaid, a blond Gentile woman, fills the bathtub for me. In the soap box and in the closet are roaches. A strife-torn night in dreams and a grayish morning. The outside was stopped by the curtains. Crowds of people with rubbed out faces. A few old cars. Awful cold. Fog.

How to leave the room and go into that reality? How to be a "tourist" in it?

Wroclaw. In the display windows rows of laundry soap in coarse packages. Cooperative restaurants smelling of cabbage and sweat. In the festival offices full ashtrays, organizers with sleepless

know that the pure prayer should be pure improvisation, that is, pure innovation, without any book, at the
same time, we know that we need a book, the code of
gestures, a language, and so on and so forth.... And
why was I in advance paralyzed at the idea that I should
have to speak? Well, given the fact that I had a childhood totally different from yours, both of you. My first,
the first question which came to me was this one: can
we pray in language one doesn't understand? Which
was my experience, at first. And I was, of course
rebelling, when I was a young Jewish boy in Algeria,
and they forced me to pray in a language which was
totally unintelligible to me. But, I think that at that
moment, I understood something essential of the
prayer. One can pray without understanding the
words. The body, the gesture, etc. means also that we
have to do something. The prayer is a doing. You do
something, even if the meaning of the words remain
opaque. What matters is a gesture of the body, of the
voice, sometimes the voice, not necessarily the meaning. That's one aspect of it. So, can one pray in language
one doesn't speak or one doesn't understand? For me
Hebrew is this. And it has to do with the book too.
Because, of course, for the same reason pure prayer
should be improvised. Invented by the praying person
for herself, or for himself; for the same reason we
should pray without the book, we don't need the book.
But, we also need the book. We need, not simply a book
which contains all the sacred narrative, sacred prayers,
and the sacred text, but a book as a body. You can just
kneel and kiss a book in which there is nothing you
can understand. That's something, I think, which
belongs to the experience of the prayer. So, there are
two contradicting axioms: pure improvisation–no
improvisation. And so on and so forth.

Now, because of this contradiction, following the
thread of these contradictions, I was thinking what the
name that Michal refers to here means. It's the Name, it's

faces. And then a writer's café, in Kosciuszko Square, and it was as if I had come to a kind of Jerusalem before I was born, from the thirties, a Jerusalem I lived from books. With that blend of provincialism and culture. Waitresses dressed in black with starch aprons, newspapers in wooden frames, cigarette smoke, grave discussions about art, literature, politics, metaphysics. The soft tones of a language that is so familiar, so close. The intonations, the gestures, the excited seriousness.

An international festival—a few days of devotion to joy, before the regime returns to its everyday gray.

And I, a stranger at the celebration. Only an "alibi" for another mission, which no one in fact has assigned to me. Yes, a few addresses for it's impossible-not-to-accept-with-a-letter-to-take before setting out. Backs of houses, yards, covered with trash and rubble. Staircase supported by boards. Number 72, apartment 9A. Two old people in the doorway. A kitchen black with soot. Examining me, the letter, with a scared look.

Sneaking back to the ongoing celebration. Just so they won't find out. It's only because of sloppiness that they haven't yet arrested me.

And then, early one misty morning, wrapped in a coat, at the railroad station. Among hundreds of people in a line. Buying a ticket to Kraków with black market Zlotys…to the regions of my real trip.

Getting off the train, and simply walking into the light-flooded square, among ancient buildings, whose carved façades are sparkling in the sun. Walking among the other people on the boulevard with the autumn chestnut trees, on Planty, Mother's route to the tennis courts. Leaves struggle on my shoes. Entering the Rynek Square resounding around itself. The Renaissance arches, the Sukiennice market in the middle like an island in the heart of a lagoon of light, the breeze rising from the Virgin Mary Church…. All those names, with a soft *r*, as I ("wonderful child!": the only two words I understood in the foreign language) would a name, and it's also the name of name, the nominal name. It's also calling as the naming: naming, calling, the act, the performative act of calling the addressee. Now, of course, as Michal rightly emphasized a moment ago, when we pray we address someone who is present or not present, so that each time we address someone, we call someone; addressing is not simply just saying something; I may say something without explicitly addressing someone. When I address some-one, each time I address someone there is some prayer involved. But does that mean that prayer is everywhere? Because we have the idea that every time we address the other, on one hand there is the promise and the prayer involved, but at the same time we know that the prayer is something exceptional. The prayer must remain exceptional. I know, we know that we are not praying all the time. The prayer should be a break in the current, in the course of existence. I may speak to a lot of people, address a lot of people, involving some prayer in it, but I know that the moment of prayer, pure prayer, implies solitude, and if not solitude, an excep-tional moment in the community, so a break with this general address, to given addressees. So, in these excep-tional moments of prayer, whether they are coded in religious languages, in religious or sacred places or not, in the street, (I can pray in the street, in houses with windows, that's the definition of the house, there is no house without the window). I can pray in the desert, sometimes we think that a pure prayer doesn't need even a house with windows, but desert; we have a lot of models of prayer in the desert. So, when this break, this interruption happens in the everyday life, on the exceptional moment of prayer, we are going back to the name, to the name of name, to the Jewish God who has, in a sense, a number of names, a nameless name, or a placeless place, and so on and so forth. We don't simply address someone, we pray to someone–God if you want, some unique one, to allow us to pray, and

JACQUES DERRIDA

accompany Mother to the nightly suppers on an aunt's balcony, with a smell of down comforters and the saltiness of the sea air on hot Tel Aviv nights, when friends from "there" would gather. All those names, when the conversation would climb in the foreign tremolo, and in the café downstairs, in the yard of the building, the cards would be shuffled on tables. The places frozen in slides on the wall of the high school, in commemorations held with a sudden frenzy. Places that were stopped in the thirties, with an amazing look of some Jew who came on the camera by mistake.... The warm-cool air caresses the fur of my coat, my face, moves the parasols over the flower vendor's booths.

The road rises to a high hill overlooking the city and the Vistula River. Above, the Wawel Castle covered in ivy burning with autumn leaves. And here, on the slope, along the banks of the Vistula, the way to Paulinska Street, Mother's street.

The three o'clock twilight lingers and softens. Mothers with babies in buggies at the river. (Mothers and babies? Still? Here?) Paulinska Street. On the secret side of the street the wall of a convent, and behind it fruit trees. Someone passes by on the corner. A woman in a heavy coat and old boots. Number eight. The staircase floored with blue tiles. A list of tenants in fountain pen. First floor on the left–a strange name. The door is locked. On the first floor a balcony. Closed glass doors, covered with lace curtains.

To throw a stone at them mischievously, a schoolbag on the back and stockings stretched up to the knee? As I walked there, dressed carefully by Mother, among the children giggling at my different clothes. To sit down at a steaming lunch, close to the breath of forefathers I never saw? Only crumbs of medicines and old lipsticks in the drawers of the aunt who died. That silence. The quiet of houses. Take a picture? A picture of air? Quiet. Across the street, in the convent garden, a bell rings. Children pour out of the gates of the school, climb on the fences, chew on apples.

Spotted façades and the street spins. Not far from there, Kazimierz, the Jewish quarter. The soot of trams on the doorsills of that's something which is very often said in *The Name*: "my Lord open my lips." I pray the Lord that He allow me to pray. I don't pray the Lord for just asking this or that, but I pray for Him or Her, for the Unique One, to free my prayer, to allow me to pray. That's why it's a prayer and an order at the same time: be the one who allows me to pray. So, be the addressee, be the addressee of my prayer, and allow me to pray. It's praying after the prayer—*prier après la prière*—which is the prayer before the prayer, the prayer for the prayer.

It's as you said, the invention of the addressee. The invention of the naming, this means calling; calling the addressee: please be the addressee. So, I am not, I should not be sure that the addressee is here, and I even have to imply that the addressee might not be here. And might never be here. Please be here, open my lips. So the prayer of the prayer, the prayer which is encrypted or included in the prayer is this address to an invisible addressee, God is perhaps not present, I don't know, I'm not sure of that, I'm not sure. Michal said that in the Jewish prayer we "produce" the God, so to speak; we make the God present, so that the presence of God depends on the prayer. Yes, yes, and possibly no. Possibly no. If we were sure that at the other end of the prayer God would show up, and that we produce the addressee, that wouldn't be a prayer. The possibility that God remains eternally absent, that there might be no addressee at the other end of my prayer is the condition of the prayer. If I was sure that my prayer would be received by some addressee, there would be no prayer. So, that's why I would go so far as to say there should be a moment of atheism in the prayer. The possibility that the God doesn't answer, doesn't exist. And I pray God that He, but that's up to Him, that He be there. But the possibility for Him not to listen to, not to respond to His name, is included in the essence of the prayer. If you want to pray, if you think you have to know how to pray, to learn how to pray, you have to the houses. In the windows of the reform synagogue, the "Temple," spiderwebs, and in the yard, a tangle of weeds. In the alley of one of the houses is a blurred sign in Yiddish, "Prayer House." The big synagogue is empty and whitewashed. Turned into a museum. Only a guard passes by like a shadow along the walls, and two fragments of tiles from back then are embedded in the entrance.

It's late now. I wander along the track to the cemetery. Here at least I am sent by permission, to an address that does exist, to the graves of the family. The gate is closed. There is no one to ask. Everything is closed.

An evening full of mist. Suddenly the trams are hurrying. The voices of the flower vendors in the Rynek are swallowed up in the fog. To go to the reserved hotel? In Kraków? Like going to a hotel in Tel Aviv instead of returning home. The desk clerk scurries up to help: "Yes, of course, Madam, here's the bus schedule to Auschwitz. From the town of Oswiecim, you have to go on foot a bit."

On the table at the entrance are old newspapers. Two elderly lady tourists are interested in a jazz festival that may not take place.

And there, at the foot of the stairs, on the way to the room, the movement that had swept me up ever since early morning stops. No, just not to return alone to the gigantic radio in the strange room! I buttoned the coat and went out in pursuit of a dubious rumor that was given to me. Slawskowska Street. *Maybe.*

And indeed, in the dark, in Yiddish, among the artisans' signs, a small address: "Mordechai Gvirtig Culture Club." A door at the edge of a yard. A doorman sits at the entrance. And in the depths, in the gloom, a few frozen figures are playing cards, gazing vacantly behind the wooden frames of newspapers. "Israel!" the doorman sits up straight, leads me with sudden importance to the "board" room. Five wrinkled faces rise up to me: "Israel!" They sit me down in the middle, following my efforts in a mixture of basic German, a few words in Yiddish, and gestures. They nod at length in deep wonder at every word, assault one another in noisy arguments. Finally, they answer together, in a strange chorus: "Ha! Yes, Poser's accept the hypothesis that you may pray for no one, for nothing. Michal told us about the three possible semantic roots of words for prayer in Hebrew, and I think, of course, that the two last ones—to plea, to request, to sentence, to judge—are really secondary, let's say. The most essential to me is the first root which means to wait, to hope, because it's not a way of hoping for this, or looking for that, but hoping for the prayer to happen. For the prayer to happen. I might not be sure that I am praying. I am never sure that this is an authentic prayer. Not only because I am not sure that the other might respond, or might be an authentic addressee, listening to me, but I'm not sure that what I'm doing now is praying. I'm not, I should never be sure of that. And that's why this depends on the fact that the prayer is a performative act, I would say in speech-act theory. It's not a contemplative act; you don't say "this is that." It's a call. It's an event which consists in doing what we say, that is calling. And when I perform such a call, I, the condition for the call to remain a call is that I won't be sure that this is a call. That's why there is something trembling, some tremor within a prayer. There is no quiet prayer. Because there is an anxiety about the authenticity of the prayer. And I'm not the one who can decide about the authenticity of the prayer. Only the other one can decide. And the other one is just a question mark. It's not just a question mark, but a possibility which remains a possibility.

Now, again, if you go back to this contradiction in the body of the prayer, a contradiction that should remain what it is, if you'd solve the problem of contradiction there's no prayer any more. If you go back to this contradiction that the prayer should be improvised and nevertheless quoted and coded, and dictated and controlled and so on and so forth, then the prayer should be as you say, I am quoting you here, "old new", it's always old new. It's always old new, as the old new synagogue in Prague. It must be new, because each time

JACQUES DERRIDA

daughter! Poser and Abeles," they nod: "Buttons, Buttons!" "Yes, buttons," I affirm; "a button factory." "The Hebrew High School," I continue. "Yes, the high school. Now a Polish technical school." The Christian cook serves me a sandwich with a lot of bread and a cup of tea. They dismiss her with the superiority of a bygone age, and urge me: "Eat, eat." For a moment, they go back to their business. The "chairman" is dictating a petition to the "secretary" about the cultural situation. To whom? On behalf of whom? Still? Like those stencilled pages in cellars and photographs of paled-faced choirs that were presented every Holocaust Memorial Day in the glass cabinets of the school. I attempt to explain; they will certainly understand that it's impossible to get on the bus and simply ask the driver in a foreign language to tell me where to get off for Auschwitz. They certainly have their own ways of getting there. And indeed, it turns out that tomorrow, a "delegation of rabbis from America" is about to come, and they will go in a special bus. When will they arrive? When will they go? Where are they now? Impossible to know. Got to wait.

I want to sneak away from them now, back to the big square. To go into an anonymous café with drunkards. To be swallowed up there. But they hang onto me, wrapped up in their coats, accompany me to the hotel. Argue with outbursts of rancor, finally declare that the "secretary" will come to "guide me" tomorrow morning. They all press around, shake my hand. Downtrodden faces. So small. In threadbare coats.

In the room the suitcase is waiting, with a few things. Makeup, passport. Will have to go on and move it. Impossible to hide in the suffocation under the blanket.

The next morning, before I have time to ponder the other world in my dreams, the "secretary" is already here, dragging me with a soft limbed domination. Turning me around in dark streets, getting on and off trams, talking incessantly in the incomprehensible language, as if to herself. And I plod behind her, bending down to her, making an effort.

it should be a new prayer, for a new moment, "I am different." This book is also about forgiveness, of course,
repentance and forgiveness. There would be a lot to say
about this, but she quotes a number of times these
statements saying; "I am different now, I'm different";
there is the one who confesses and who repents, and
says, "I am different." I am different from the one who
committed these sins and so on, so forth. What does
that mean, "I am different" when someone says "I am
different"? It's a strange sentence, is it possible to say
"I am different"? If I say "I am different from myself
yesterday", it means that I'm not different. If I say "I", I
can't say "I'm different." In the case of pure confession,
pure repentance, "I am different" might be possible;
the "I" who says "I am different" is a different "I."
So, each time I pray, I must imply "I am different." It's a
different prayer, it's new, I don't simply repeat like a
recording, I am not just repeating the prayer I've
learned, or rituals. I'm just inventing a poem, that's
what prayer is–a poem. A prayer is a language that you
have to invent, improvise and invent. So, I am different
when I pray. But at the same time, because of these
contradictions, I must keep the memory, keep some
memory, and repeat something, where the body comes
back. The body, when you kneel, you kneel or, when
you join your hands and so on. You have a feeling that
the body must subject, must submit itself to some prior
law, or something prior to the act of the prayer. So, this
contradiction of the "I am different" must remain intact.
Making the prayer impossible. And a prayer must
remain impossible. If by praying I was just doing what
is possible, what I can do, (every day I, many people do
that, they stand up, they put on the tallith and they pray;
it's possible): this is not a prayer. The prayer should do
what is impossible, and for this to take into account, or
not to take into account, to keep intact the contradiction. I am different. I am inventing a new "I." I am a
new "I."

MICHAL GOVRIN

LETTER from REGIONS OF DELUSION

In Kazimierz, on the bench across from the synagogue, the doorman of the "Mordechai Gvirtig Culture Club" and two old men are already waiting for me. It's not clear if they're beggars or rabbis. They came to welcome the "American delegation." The doorman waving as he approaches, "Yes, yes!" One of the old men hurries me, opens the gates of the ancient synagogue of Rabbi Moshe Isserlish. For a minute, a separate hush. The figures that follow in my wake remain beyond the fence. A small building whose heavy walls are leaning, and a white courtyard. Inside the synagogue, there is still a warmth among the wooden benches, around the Ark of the Covenant. On the tables are old prayer books. Black letters. And in the small enclosure crows land on the ancient tombstones sunk in mist. For a moment the past seems to continue with all its softness, without any obstacle, in that distant murmur, up to the morning covered with mist, to me.

And the doorman is already rushing me hysterically; he arranged with the gatekeeper of the Miodowa cemetery to be there, to open the gate. Hurry, hurry, got to get back in time for the "delegation of rabbis!" And thus, in single file, the doorman limping, the muscular Christian gatekeeper on his heels, and I behind them, we march between long rows of sunken, shattered gravestones, covered with mold. Names, names. I recite to them the names I've managed to dredge up from my memory, "Poser, Mendel, Groner." Tombstones in long rows whose edges vanish in mist and piles of fallen leaves. Many strange names. Don't find. A Christian woman with legs swathed in bandages rinses the graves with boiling water, raises her head wrapped in a turban to us: "Yes, Groner, I saw it once… maybe there." I still hold on, persist in reading the names, seeking under piles of leaves. But the limping doorman and the gatekeeper behind him are already hurrying out. We didn't find. No maps. No books. No witnesses. Mission impossible. Only a delusion of a mission. And time is limited.

Meanwhile on the bench the number of idlers and "rabbis" waiting for the "American delegation" had grown. According to the doorman, they are already in Kraków and will arrive very soon.

But, let us go back for just one more second, to JACQUES DERRIDA the question of forgiveness and repentance, which is at the center of this book that you should read; if I ask for forgiveness by saying "I am different," then it means that I am not the one who, I'm presently not the one who was responsible for the crime. I am changed. So, the scene of forgiveness as essentially associated with prayer is this paradox too. I must remain the same at the same time. I must remain the same. By saying that I am different I must remain the same in order to take the responsibility for what I'm asking for forgiveness. So, in the prayer I should be at the same time the same and different. And this contradiction is embodied in the prayer. This contradiction is precisely, I think, what happens in the prayer and should remain, let's say, as intense as possible. Inventing and repeating, improvising while following the rules. Inventing the addressee while respecting the absolute transcendence of the addressee. If I say, the way Michal said, "Jews produce the addressee," that would be a blasphemy, of course. God doesn't need, God doesn't need a prayer to be…but I must at the same time produce God. I must, the address of the addressor must produce the addressee while respecting the absolute transcendence, the absolute pre-existence, the absolute otherness of the addressee. The addressee doesn't depend on my prayer, but my prayer invents my relationship with this other. So, it is this double bind, that I wanted just to emphasize.

Thank you. Actually this morning I was thinking of what DAVID SHAPIRO Roman Jakobson said when he was hit by the automobile, he shouted "Help!" in forty-seven languages. I was thinking of this shout today and we've been using the sense of the addressee (and I even wrote a little poem about this addressee). We often think of Jakobson's great schema and *foregrounding*: one or two parts of the linguistic situation. I was thinking this morning as I heard dogs moaning, and pigeons—pigeons like dogs and dogs like pigeons—that

Maybe you can find out in the hotel when they'll arrive? No, impossible to know. I break away from the doorman, tell him I'll come back in a little while, he should beg the rabbis of the delegation to wait, and I hurry to Wawel Castle, for the visit that was arranged. On the streets people in gray coats, buses, trams. You can even eat an apple. The body goes on functioning over the abyss between the worlds. And when I come back from the royal palace, from the halls with waxed floors whose walls are covered with embroidered tapestries of feast and forest, devoured by torments of treason, I run down the slope carpeted with fallen leaves, back to Kazimierz, to my Jews. From the end of the street, the doorman stumbles toward me. He drops his hands in a gesture of dismissal: "Well, the American delegation… a call came that they didn't leave America. Well, the fog, they didn't leave America."

Empty. No one there. Even the idlers who were waiting on the bench have gone home.

Entrusted with the last mission, the doorman rushes me into the community organization offices. Second floor, a smell of boiled potatoes, a few old people with tin plates and spoons. Even the bright light filtering from the shutters doesn't bring the scene in the room any closer. Around an enormous table sit the activists of the "congregation," their chins leaning on their hands, and their crutches leaning on the chairs. A few old portraits on the walls. At the head of the table, Mr. Jacobovitch, an irascible Jew, head of the community organization. The mutual curiosity dies out after a few sentences, and after I am given the travel arrangements, I slip out impolitely. I also flee from the kosher meal of mashed potatoes on a tin plate and the ritual washing of the hands in a stained sink, to Sukiennice Square, to the light, to the fancy café with red velvet chairs and torte powdered like the cheeks of Polish women. Here you can shout aloud that maybe everything is a delusion, that maybe there never were Jews here.

And it was as if a shout burst out of me in the evening, at the performance of "The Night of November Ninth" by Wyspianski, directed by Swinarski. Mythic characters singing against a back-this cry of help is part of the, what Jakobson would call, the addressor and dominantly emotive sense of the prayer. We also have a kind of complexity, this contradictory prayer, like "primary antithetical words," this *cleaving*, and I thought that, like poetry, prayer is this very strangely complex object, from a petition to a intercession, to a celebration, to a contemplation. It's a situation which would foreground *almost everything*, and in which it is true that the addressee has slipped away, but even so the slipped-away addressee is part of the grand pathos of what is a prayer. Emily Dickinson says in one of her poems, "prayer is the little implement through which men reach, where presence is denied them." Sounds like she had read you –during the Civil War in 1862. They *fling their speech* in God's ear. And then with pathos, with Emily Dickinson's dashes and discontinuities, she says, "If then he hear," I was very interested in this line, "If then he hear," she stops, and *she just says*, "This sums up the apparatus, comprised in prayer," so there's this grand pathos. Heschel talks of God in search of man. I just wanted to thank you both because I thought this morning, writing a little poem about being a dog, and praying, was about the best that "we" can do. We reinitiate. My own grandfather went from Minsk to Smolensk, finally to Boston, Newark, to Harlem to research jazz, and you feel: what he did learn? A cantillation or the trope canonic and unconventional. I thought, since we both love the Angelus Silesius, of this great question that you seem to raise, as in Artaud, like a system of cruelty, as Nietzsche said of all religions, "The hole in my heart cries to the hole that is God's; which is deeper?." It's a strange couplet. And reading your book, I keep coming upon that as an extraordinary question. Something like the abyss of Baudelaire's *Pascal*. So, I'm glad that we've left this, not exactly in the interrogative; I think that the grammar of prayer is strange enough, and truly uncanny. Prayer is not at home and is for the homeless.

The architect Peter Eisenman said to me when I first met him, "Of course, we have nothing in common." I said, ground of a burning horizon. The tricolored flag of the revolution waves over the stage, and the audience is galvanized. A moment of naked yearning for freedom is revealed, of metaphysical emotion, a moment of a personal world despite the constant oppression. Something so familiar, so close in temperament, in gestures. Such belonging. Belonging?

An old car. The shaved nape of the driver's neck stuck in a cap. Poplar trees, autumn fields. I am in the back seat, huddled in my coat. On the way to Auschwitz.

And perhaps you should be silent about that trip. Not talk about the yellow flowers, the gravel in the sun, the chatter of the Polish cleaning women who laughingly point out to me that my trousers are unstitched. My trousers? On what side of the barrier?

How to write you about the heavy marching in an attempt to grasp something through the remnants of constructions—as from archaeological digs of thirty, not two thousand years ago. To understand the chasm separating sanity and madness with barbed-wire fences. The house beyond the fence, half a mile away, was always there, with the same smoke in the chimney and the same geranium pots behind the curtains. And here?

How to write about the dark steps with a group of Polish high school students on them. The wall of liquidations between two blocs. A barred window. A few fallen leaves scattered on the sill. Expressionless walls in the gas chambers, the iron doors of the ovens. Polish sky. Between the chambers, in the corridors, photographs and numbers. Printed columns of names. And the silence of another morning, now. As when I held my breath, a girl of six or seven, in the schoolyard for a whole minute, through the whole siren, so that I'd be dizzy when I intoned the words, *six million.*

How to write you about the forced march through the tremendous extents of Birkenau Camp. About the dampness still standing in the abandoned blocs, between those three-tiered wooden bunks, and the straw sacks on the dirt floor. How to imagine Mother within that silent madness. Mother. A shaven head in

"What do you mean?" He said, "You can choose anything, I am limited." I said, "Oh?" He said, "Yes, I can't…poetry is…it's rhyme, it's this…" I said, "I can choose anything?" And I thought today again about the grammar of poetry; even after a first word I can not choose *anything*; it is already a grammar. Law and story divide the Jewish experience like dispersion and unity. Michal has said that Jerusalem was like a woman whose private parts were being fought over. And my friend in Los Angeles asked me today to ask you about *the city*, the city of prayer. And the specter of the city. And, I don't know if we have time to talk here, but I thought at least there'd be a *framing device*, a parergon of questions. John Hejduk loves very often to end things saying, "No questions," and that is a kind of authority. But would you have some questions that you might ask, not me, but Michal and Jacques, two visitors? If you are willing to stay. Gertrude Stein says, "There is never all of any visit." Would you be willing to hear some questions?

Yes, of course.   JACQUES DERRIDA

So I throw it open; I know when I am in an audience what   DAVID SHAPIRO
I'm really waiting for is for "them" to stop and for me to
speak, and some people say, "That's what's happened to
God, you know he's not hiding, he's waiting for us to look
for him a little more closely." Kafka said "There is only a
spiritual world, which gives us no comfort." That was one
of the great prayers I thought. So, your hands are also
possible. Like a prayer. Sir, yes?

It was very interesting to me about the possible and the   TAMAS SZALCZER
impossible, in prayer. The possibility of addressing. And, to   *STUDENT*
me, this possible and impossible, since they are the same,
denies faith in a way. On the other hand, Michal expressed
space and body in a degree that was almost shocking. And
space and the impossible…so this space creates a very strange
space, that, together within the impossibility…. But, if I need
to seek the impossible or possible, out from this space, then
space sustains a possibility of faith. So I am just curious about

nights of hallucinations, nights among packed bodies. How to put Mother into one of the gigantic photos placed along the railroad track. How to force myself to imagine her in this emptiness?

Polish earth. Small autumn flowers. The driver waits. Dozes in the sun in the car.

And maybe all the questions are not right. For it's impossible to understand. Not even at the end of the journey to this stage set. Impossible to understand without the fear of death that catches the breath, without the palpable threat on the flesh. Impossible to grasp death from all the hundreds of photos. Maybe only the heaps of empty shoes are still hovering between life and death. There I finally recited the *Kaddish*. *Kaddish* over heaps of shoes.

And maybe all the questions start only after the shoes also crumble. Beyond the crazy stage set of death, which will always remain incomprehensible. And maybe all the questions begin only with the silent emptiness of now. How to go on living in a world that has turned into the enemy. With the fear stamped in the blood. With the constant paranoia. "*Arbeit macht frei.*" How to live within the world and outside it. In the flow of its life and in the flow of other life and eternity. How to go on nevertheless believing in man, how to take the beloved head in the arms.

In the afternoon light, trivial thoughts pass through the head. Impossible to pretend suffering; that would be hypocrisy. Impossible to go back to the past—clinging or accusing—that would be the triumph of the past. There is no escape from the constant questions to be asked now, impossible to flee from them to the images frozen in the photos.

And in Warsaw, in the Ghetto, there aren't even any ruins where the imagination can take hold for a moment. There are no stones that are emitted outside of time. Only concrete blocks built a few feet above the ground, above the ruins and the mounds of corpses that weren't even cleared away. To hold your head in your hands and shout. Life goes on. Cars in parking lots, a few poplar trees on the sidewalks. And that emptiness. Only the lip service of this possible or impossible addressee: How? What kind of space, or how does it recreate space or can this space be seen as faith? It is because I saw the space and body in the poems and the reading as something graspable, or attainable, something that is shaped. But, the possible and the impossible; there is so powerful a contradiction in that which creates some kind of terrible emotional state.

Michal will tell you what she means by space and even if it is a graspable space. I'm not sure, but she will tell you. As for me, if I understood your question correctly, I wouldn't say that what I said about the impossible, impossible and possible, is a denial of faith. I would say exactly the opposite: if I was sure that the addressee would be responding or would be present, there would be no faith required. The faith, the act of pure faith implies precisely that I can not, that I should not and could not, be sure of the possibility. I should and could not be sure of the existence, of the presence. Because it is impossible for me to know—because of the gap between faith and knowledge, because I cannot know and I cannot perceive the presence of the other as such —the act of faith is absolutely required.

JACQUES DERRIDA

I can only thank Jacques for being here, for answering in a way that for me has always been a stirring definition of what faith is. And linked to the impossibility. As for the body and space, I cannot add much…I think that there are moments when the prayer itself is becoming a closed space, a prayer with no faith. Faith in that definition is being at the edge of not-knowing, with an intention [*Kavanah*] that always has to be renewed. There are few chapters of Psalms that start with the expression: "new song" [שיר חדש/*shir hadash*]. Malbim said in his commentary, "What does it mean a new song; what is this total improvisation, this invention? It's the song of facing an unknown space, something that has not existed before; totally new." And what

MICHAL GOVRIN

a memorial with the pathos of socialist realism, and a Jewish museum behind the building of the Communist party. The director of the museum and his secretary, two Jews with bowed heads, show me a building excavation out the window. "Here was the great synagogue of Warsaw." And the cleaning woman smiles like an accomplice in a crime, points at the exit to the guest book full of emotional comments. Gray cement boulevards and gigantic statues of soldiers with forged chins. Impossible to believe that there was once a different life here. Only in the nationalized *Desa* stores are scores of Jewish objects. Hanukkah lamps, synagogue menorahs, spice boxes. Objects with price tags. No, there is nowhere to return. The whole thing is only a delusion. Deceptions of the imagination. In my head, crushed fragments of all the artistic creations resound, the assemblies, the recitations that tried to convey the other reality to me, and they only increase the distance.

The rain doesn't let up. An awful cold penetrates the clothes, makes you shiver. Warsaw–a gray horizon by day, and gray in the pale neon lights at night. The trip seems like an illusion, like opening the camp gate and being outside. The unbearable loneliness, the unrelenting stifling.

Only the friendship of my acquaintances, Polish theater people, supports me in hours before the departure. Figures between reality and dream. Alicia in her theatrical clothes, waving her hands like a Chekhov character. And Andrzej with ironical humor, in fragments of literary French, with the credo from Communism to the surrealism of Witkiewicz. Fervent confessions in small apartments, when tomorrow is unknown, and only the dream is left. Like the awakening appreciation for Bruno Schulz, thirty years after he perished, like worshipping the theater, the word spoken from the stage, received with a sigh. Like the clandestine grasping of Catholicism.

Childhood memories extend between Mediterranean summers and alleys in northern cities, woven in the dreams of Polish romantic literary heroes, shrouded in the sounds of the language, and open accounts of the blood of the dead. Life in a pre-time is about time? We have not spoken about time, we could have dealt with that issue these two hours. How much are we projected into "unknown" time; the extremity of not knowing what will come? So, when you are at the edge of not knowing, it's a very difficult position. Yet, when you lose this edge of not knowing that's the end, the decadence, of prayer; when the prayer closes back to an assured space, assured address and assured time. Prayer is improvisational, although maybe it's recited from a book. At least by the fact that you, in the way you say it, you are not sure that the space and time are there. And as for the body, yes, you see God from the body. The body is there. But how, in what way, how to move the body into meaning, how to create from that body a scripture, what language the body speaks at that moment, is also an open question. And if I did work with space here, I was going from a prayer which would be a closed space into a prayer which would be the shattering of the space, and being not only in a room with windows but maybe in a constant/temporary, non-structure, which is moving, as if you are in virtual reality, that you walk and you create and yet you don't know where you will be. Kind of an architecture which is never certain, which is never there, and yet you need to have faith in order to go forward. And once you go forward, with enough insolence, to overtake, or overcome your fear then something is created, but you could never have known that in advance, because then it wouldn't be that act of creation. There is always this ambiguity of the border of not knowing as a premise for creation or for praying or being in a space, or creating ongoing space.

One of the things that interests me in rabbinic tradition is the Hasidic idea that prayer should be prepared for in an hour or more, *in the open fields*. There used to be a canonic prescription, not just Hasidic, of those who could get to the crisis of prayer. And I am also thinking of Rimbaud's

DAVID SHAPIRO

always present, in the double look at all the places. Always through the other place I belong to, where you don't come on journeys. A wiped-out place, condemned to delusion, where I will never be able to rest the wandering of existences.

With relief, I finally board the train. Sleeping cars that came from Moscow with a conductor in an undershirt and a stifling of sweat and orange peels. A twenty-four-hour trip to Paris, like a day of fasting. To another world? At midnight, the train passes the East Berlin station. Signs in Gothic script: "Welcome to the Democratic Capital." On the platform is a white line three feet from the cars. Soldiers in riding boots with German shepherds and submachine guns are standing at regular intervals. A patrol of two soldiers goes through the train. Another patrol checks between the wheels with flashlights, and another one marches on the roofs of the cars. Maybe someone has succeeded in escaping. A white line, soldiers, and a train. Only the site of madness or freedom has changed.

Back in Paris. The clear sky, department-store advertising instead of propaganda slogans. Quiet. The silence of the room. And that drawn orbit of life where you two are so close at hand. "Flesh of my flesh."

Beloved Father and Mother, I press you to my heart, and once again am gathered in your arms.

sense for the poet; we speak of Rimbaud as one of the great seers of the impossible, he has it within *Season in Hell*: the impossible representation of purity, as by derangement, a prayerful method.

So, I think that he was one of the great inventors, though it turns out, of course, that he was very much within a code from the Bible to Whitman in translation to himself, but Rimbaud is obviously one of those who we can really think of as being tormented by this, in the freshest way, by this fresh torment of trying *to name* something. The name for Rimbaud is a task. He says, "The first adventure, *le premiere aventure, un fleur que me dit son nom*: a flower told me her name." An extraordinary sense of someone reaching out to this Adam and telling the name. I just mention Rimbaud to give us a sense of the terrible, which, I think, is lodged inside this novel, in which it is so difficult to think of languages that it becomes a fresh assemblage of many languages. Meyer Schapiro once said to me, "How's your Aramaic?", to which my Father said, "You should have said, it's pretty good with the Kaddish." And, so we have, in our great Aramaic prayer, a very strange music of linguistic incomprehension, of uncertainty. We honor Rimbaud for his uncertainty. Almost at the edge of giving up. I had friends who said, "Maybe in Africa he had a child and wrote other poems." We have to be satisfied with the greater spectacle—not spectacle—but festival. The festival of Rimbaud who was able to get so much closer to freshness and to purity and naming. We stand amazed and astonished at Rimbaud, or at Rabbi Heschel who said to someone very early in the morning, "What have you learned today?", and the man said, "Very little, actually, Rabbi." He said, "Haven't you seen the trees, praying, he meant *dovenning*, twisting metaphorically in prayer. Nature itself prays to the seer.

So, another question. Matti had a question.

I must.... There are two sentences that call for an explanation. One is: "*Adonai Sefatai Tiphtach U'phi Yagid Tehilatecha*, My

MATTI MEGGED
VISITOR

CIRCUMFESSION *PERIPHASES*
3:I–VIII

Lord open my lips; and my mouth will say your praise." It's not a question, my lips will say your praise, honor, or glory, whatever you call it. And the other one is: *"Sh'ma Ysra'el Adonai Eloheinu Adonai Echad*, Hear, O Israel! God is our Lord, God is one." How do you read that?

You can read it in two totally different ways. One is, "Sh'ma Ysra'el," Listen Israel. God is our Lord, God is one. Or, "Sh'ma le Ysra'el," Listen to Israel. God, Hear to Israel. Listen to Israel. How do you explain it?

This is a historical moment, because the meaning of Sh'ma Ysra'el…I've been waiting for this moment.   JACQUES DERRIDA

Yes, and I want to repeat for the people in the back to know that the canonic prayer Sh'ma Ysra'el which has been the question, if I can phrase it, like the question from Apollinaire: how to punctuate this? Whether you have, and maybe we can leave it with the uncertainty, but this canonic prayer on the lips of the great martyrs, is it, "Hear, O Israel!", or a question "Listen to Israel?." This is the question of the addressor and the addressee which Michal has pronounced.   DAVID SHAPIRO.

We don't have to decide. I am thinking of what Rimbaud and Apollinaire would think of being recontextualized here.   JACQUES DERRIDA

I don't think that there is one answer and I'll have a hundred answers. There is an uncertainty of how to understand it, which is maybe at the core of the story of Rabbi Akiba. What did he mean at that moment when he died with the words of the Sh'ma on his lips? Was that a total blasphemy; showing through his act who's the One in "God is One," in prolonging the word Ehad—One—until he expired while saying it? Did "one" mean cleavage in the one? His cleavage? Or was it a total human independence; his doing his job, fulfilling that extreme *Mitzva* [prescription], and maybe saying: Listen,   MICHAL GOVRIN

Consign them here, but why I wonder, confide to the bottom of this book what were my mother's last more or less intelligible sentences, still alive at the moment I am writing this, but already incapable of memory, in any case of the memory of my name, a name become for her at the very least unpronounceable, and I am writing here at the moment when my mother no longer recognizes me, and at which, still capable of speaking or articulating, a little, she no longer calls me and for her and therefore for the rest of her life I no longer have a name, that's what's happening, and when she nonetheless seems to reply to me, she is presumably replying to someone who happens to be me without her knowing it, if knowing means anything here, therefore without my knowing henceforth any more clearly myself who will have asked her such and such a question like the other day in Nice when I asked her if she was in pain ("yes") then where, it was February 5, 1989, she had, in a rhetoric that could never have been hers, the audacity of this stroke about which she will, alas, never know anything, no doubt knew nothing, and which piercing the night replies to my question: "I have a pain in my mother," as though she were speaking *for* me, both in my direction and in my place, although in the apparently amnesiac confusion in which she is ending her days the memory of *her* mother is very present to her, and although she looks more and more like her, I mean like my grandmother, a woman just as attentive to her appearance, her clothing, her makeup and her manners, then the evening of the same day, when she was alone with me in that house and I was in a different room, she had several times successively exposed herself naked, having nervily torn off the clothes that were hampering

O God. You listen, You are my addressee, despite all? What was that legacy, said in his body? What does that mean? No, I don't have an answer. And I think that these open questions are what make us work.

Just a short commentary. The fact that we cannot decide in this case, that we cannot interpret it in a decisive manner, perhaps has something to do with the prayer. That is, a prayer should be interrupted. There is a moment of preparation; we have to be ready for the prayer. But, on the other side, when we pray, the prayer shouldn't come to an end, because if the prayer is complete it is not prayer. So, the address to the other must remain interrupted. The interruption is the mode of our relation to the other. The prayer should remain interrupted. Not simply because someone has interrupted the prayer but because the meaning of the prayer remains undecidable. Must remain suspended. I'm not sure what I'm saying when I pray. So, this is the interruption; not because I'm physically interrupted, but because I'm not sure of what my words mean. Because the other will tell me what I mean. The meaning of what I say is in the hands or in the ears of the other. So there is an essential interruption within the prayer because, because it depends on the other. On the response of the other.

JACQUES DERRIDA

My son said fearfully before his Bar-mitzvah, "And there will be not only no vowels, but no punctuation in the Torah." And we think of that mode. There's a moment when Apollinaire leaves out the punctuation. I have a terrible thought of a poet who, in a recent translation of Alcools, *put in* the punctuation! And I thought this would be like going back to one of the great cubist paintings like *Ma jolie*, and somehow taking away the uncertain. Bill Rubin asked Picasso, and he said this was one of the smartest things Picasso ever told him: "Was there always an object when you were painting?" Picasso said, "No"–I

DAVID SHAPIRO

her in her bed, then as soon as I asked her why she replied to me, in just as *improbable* a way for anyone who had known her: "Because I'm attractive," and because she no longer articulates very clearly, her refusal to keep false teeth in not helping matters, I wonder if I had heard aright, had she said "Because I'm attractive," had she really, however true it might be, spoken such an improbable sentence, but instead of pursuing this story, I stop for a moment over this word "improbable" and over a pang of remorse, in any case over the admission I owe the reader, in truth that I owe my mother herself for the reader will have understood that I am writing for my mother, perhaps even for a dead woman and so many ancient or recent analogies will come to the reader's mind even if no, they don't hold, those analogies, none of them, for if I were here writing for my mother, it would be for a living mother who does not recognize her son, and I am periphrasing here for whomever no longer recognizes me, unless it be so that one should no longer recognize me, another way of saying, another version, so that people think they finally recognize me, but what credulity, for here's the basis of the improbable, improbable is here below the name.

am paraphrasing it, Dore Ashton is much more master of Picasso's words so, permit me this metaphrasis. He said, "it was before us, it was to the side of us, it was in back of us, it was a fragrance of an object." That is a very good statement. And the great prayers are perhaps, in that sense, before us, and to the side and after. I take it very seriously because this is a prayer with which many Jews have died. Saying this prayer, naming this prayer. It's important to realize this. I'm always dazzled how few of our students have memorized prayers. I always pray in planes, and I take many flights. I don't want to go down reading *Time* magazine, somehow, I would rather die with a *Song of David* on my lips. In Thessalonians there's a sentimental saying, "Pray without ceasing." Jews have "You will not pray over much." The Talmud says there are these maidens who were *too prayerful*, they wrecked the world. I quoted this about gender to Michal one day. At least one sage said, "I wish I could pray all day." And to be in this state, Kenneth Koch said, "The good poet learns how to get himself *into the state* of inspiration." I think what you've said is also very important to recount, *which is also the powerful*, as we end this short seminar on long prayer, because we don't want to keep Monsieur Derrida or Madame Govrin here too long. We have to decide how these things end. Kenneth Koch said, "Don't end a poem with the ocean, end it with a proper sense of endlessness." So, I am trying to think how we can cut this. Is there a question, that must be asked? Kierkegaard preferred short prayers, and we are condemned to cleave this in all senses.

There was a question here.   JACQUES DERRIDA

A question with a proper *Kavanah* or devotional sense?   DAVID SHAPIRO

My question touches a little bit on a big question of whether   LIYAT ESAKOV
the addressee exists or not. More specifically, you gave an   *STUDENT*
explanation of the word "pray", using hope, aspiration, waiting, and assuming. And I'm wondering if you necessarily

If it is invulnerable, this matrix, and some would say that that's its defect, what on earth can happen to it, from what wound is it waiting for me, me who, among other remorse with respect to my mother, feel really guilty for publishing her end, in exhibiting her last breaths and, still worse, for purposes that some might judge to be literary, at risk of adding a dubious exercise to the "writer and his mother" series, subseries "the mother's death," and what is there to be done, would I not feel as guilty, and would I not in truth *be* as guilty if I wrote here about myself without retaining the least trace of her, letting her die in the depth of another time, if I remember that December 24, 1988, when already she was hardly saying anything articulate anymore, nor apparently fitting the situation, nothing that thus seemed to answer to the normal rule of human exchange, she pronounced clearly, in the midst of confused groanings "I want to kill myself," and precisely what G. up there, very close or too late, cannot let you understand or guess, and that no doubt my writings can manifest but as though illegibly, following some rule of reading still to be formulated, is that "I want to kill myself" is a sentence of mine, me all over, but known to me alone, the mise en scene of a suicide and the fictive but oh how motivated, convinced, serious decision to put an end to my days, a decision constantly relaunched, a rehearsal which occupies the entire time of my internal theater, the show I put on for myself without a break, before a crowd of ghosts, a rite and an effusion which have a limit all the less for the fact that their invisibility is guaranteed, the very secret in which I keep this ritualized effusion, beginning with prayer and tears, and I wonder if those reading me from up there see my tears, today, those of the child about graft these words to the realm of God or whether you think that they can exist on their own–in your understanding of prayer. I mean, does hope necessarily have to do with this addressee as well?

Hope, in my definition of being prophetic, means that you are in the present, and you envision another reality; you bridge those two realities by what you would call hope–that the other reality will come into the present. Which means that you project yourself into the future. I think that might be a kind of a special definition of hope.

MICHAL GOVRIN

For this child I prayed.

MATTI MEGGED

That's a loaded sentence Matti.

MICHAL GOVRIN

I know it's loaded.

MATTI MEGGED

So, I think that, in that sense you can leave God out of the picture. And you can say that whenever future is involved, whenever you dare project yourself, prophetically, into yet an unknown future, there is faith. Because, otherwise, without this "irrational" hope, we would get paralyzed and wouldn't move.

MICHAL GOVRIN

I have a question, I agree on that, fully. And I think I understand why prayer and hope, are essentially associated. But I'm thinking of another possibility that I can't exclude. The possibility of a hopeless prayer. You may pray without any reference to the future, just to address the other, hopelessly, hopelessly: in reference only to the past. There is only repetition, no future. And, nevertheless, you pray. Is that possible? To pray hopelessly? And is it possible to pray hopelessly, not only without request, but even by giving up hope? If one agrees that there is such a possibility of prayer, a pure prayer, that is hopeless, then shouldn't we think

JACQUES DERRIDA

whom people used to say "he cries for nothing," and indeed, if they guess that my life was but a long history of prayers, and the incessant return of the "I want to kill myself" speaks less the desire to put an end to my life than a sort of compulsion to overtake each second, like one car overtaking another, doubling it rather, overprinting it with the negative of a photograph already taken with a "delay" mechanism, the memory of what survived me to be present at my disappearance, interprets or runs the film again, and already I catch them out seeing me lying on my back, in the depth of my earth, I mean, they understand everything, like the geologic program, except that I have lived in prayer, tears and the imminence at every moment of their survival, terminable survival from which "I see myself live" translates "I see myself die," I see myself dead cut from you in your memories that I love and I weep like my own children at the edge of my grave, I weep not only for my children but for all my children, why only you, my children?

that finally the essence of prayer has something to do with this despair, with this hopelessness? The pure prayer doesn't ask for anything, not even for the future. Now, I can imagine the response to this terrible doubt: that, even in that case, if I pray hopelessly, there is a hope in the prayer. I would hope, at least, for someone sharing my prayer or someone listening to my prayer, or someone understanding my hopelessness and my despair and so in that case there is, nevertheless, a hope and a future. But, perhaps not. Perhaps not. At least *perhaps*, this is for me also, a terrible condition of the prayer.

I think that I'll answer you in your own terms; that maybe these are the two conditions of prayer–the hope and the hopelessness. I think that when there's sheer hope there is no need for prayer. I mean, what for? What for? You just glide triumphantly towards the future. In a "hopeful, Wall Street" way, no problem, everything is smooth. I think that you don't need to pray. What for? The prayer needs this condition of hopelessness and, moments of total despair. But then, in those moments of hopelessness, you can ask again: why to pray? I think you could ask the question of both—why to pray when you are hopeful and why to pray when you are despairing.

MICHAL GOVRIN

When I pray I am always asking myself "Why do I pray?"

JACQUES DERRIDA

This leads us to Kafka, who always seems so legalistic and criminal that he has a taste for the darkest moments of the Talmud. There is a tale in the Talmud of a dispute, when the great sages debate whether it was better for man to be born or not to be born. I always read this passage in great fear. And the answer is that they decided it was better for him not to be born. There is very little commentary about this. And it is a comfortless situation.

DAVID SHAPIRO

Deep in the history of penitence, from repentance to regret and contrition, from public avowal with expiation to private avowal and confession, from public reconciliation to reparation then to absolution, between blood and water, and baptism, and white and red veils, Tertullian the African, the council of Latran and Saint John Nepomucenus, martyr of the secret of confession, and Saint Augustine, of whom I read that "having returned to God, he probably never confessed, in the modern sense of the word," never having had, any more than I, beyond even truth, "the opportunity to 'confess,'" which precisely does not prevent him from working at the delivery of literary confessions, i.e. at a form of theology as autobiography, I wonder, interested in the depth of the bedsore, not in writing or literature, art, philosophy, science, religion or politics but only memory and heart, not even the history of the presence of the present, I wonder what I am looking for with this machine avowal, beyond institutions, including psychoanalysis, beyond knowledge and truth, which has nothing to do with it here, beyond even the "scandalously beautiful" hypothesis of my secret name, Elie, around which the first notebooks from 1976 circled, drawing pads with thick leaves whose cover bore an *escarre*, i.e. a coat of arms with two lions, and, written on the edge of an open square the words *skizze, croquis, sketch, schizzo, schets, kpoki,* and I added by hand, in Hebrew, the word for word, מילה, pronounce it *milah*, which names the word and circumcision, trying to find out already whom at bottom Elie would have loved, from whom, "last loved face" he would have chosen to receive his name like an absolution at the end of a confession without truth, for the love of you, to make the love of you, to make what I am making

Job, Job says something like…

JACQUES DERRIDA

Yes, Scholem wrote a beautiful essay on cursing God as suicide. Rimbaud said, "Merde à Dieu", and someone said, "Think of the antagonist that he required." For a little boy to say "Merde à Dieu" on a park bench. The hopelessness and hope he was thinking. Goldstein, the great neurophysiologist says, "the loss of the abstract attitude, one of the saddest moments of the mind, is the deletion of the future tense." And I would think that one of the saddest things that happens within the madness of your character, and within the madness within parts of Kafka was something like a staging of the loss of the abstract attitude. I knew my mother was dying when she didn't read newspapers. Something terribly lost, prayer without future tense. Emily Dickinson says, "This is my letter to the world, that never wrote to me." It's true that there does seem to be lodged in the composition of prayer, something like that minimal hope when the great actor who used to play Beckett's parts, David Warrilow, would move *an inch*, and as Cézanne said, "The world would change." So, I want to thank everyone for coming, and we won't vex you with more prayers. And, I thank our visitors that come to Cooper, where John Hejduk has reminded us that the education of the architect is making sacred space.

DAVID SHAPIRO

here for the love that you would have for Elie, *amore amoris tui facio istuc,*[1] thus *"the fact that this forename was not inscribed [on my birth certificate, as were the Hebrew names of my family] (as though they wanted to hide it, still more than the other Hebrew names, placed after the others), was a though effaced, held back, signified several things mixed together: first of all that they wanted to hide me like a prince whose parentage is provisionally concealed to keep him alive (I've just thought, trying to explain this gesture to myself [my parents never talked to me about it, I never asked them about it, it remains secondary and occupies so much space here only because of the thread I have chosen to follow] that a brother died when a few months old, less than a year before my birth, between my elder brother, René [Abraham], and me. He was called Paul Moses), keep him alive until the day that his royalty could [...] be openly exercised, without risk for the precious semen; and then that I should not openly wear any Jewish sign"* (12-23-76).

[1] IN THE LOVE OF THY LOVE AM I DOING THIS (XI, I, 1).

I invent the word *dhavec* this day of Purim 5750, while Esther still lives on and for almost a year and a half, without ever being interested in this name Esther, in spite of my appeals, still less at this moment at which she is surviving the conscience of me, of her name as of mine, I lean over her budding *escarres*, "they look good" said the reassuring nurse, they are roaring in the carnage of a protest, life has always protested in my mother, and if "bad blood" will always be for me *her* expression, if from alone I have received it, heard it or learned it, from her impatient sighs, this is because I began with this fear, with being scared of her bad blood, with not wanting it, whence the infinite separation, the initial and instantaneously repeated i.e. indefinitely postponed divorce from [*d'avec*] the closest cruelty which has not that of my mother but the distance she enjoined on me from [*d'avec*] my own skin thus torn off, in the very place, along the crural artery where my books find their inspiration, they are written first in skin, they read the death sentence held in reserve on the other side of the screen for in the end since the computer I have my memory like a sky in front of me, all the succor, all the threats of a sky, the pelliculated simulacrum of another absolute subjectivity, a transcendence which I would finally do with as she would like, she who wants my death, *"the sublime scission, the bottomless bet: to learn how to love—that cannot fail to repeat one and many closed-up rents, open again the wound of circumcision, analyze that form of secret, the 'my life' which is neither a content to be hidden nor an inside of the solitary self but hangs on the partition between two absolute subjectivities, two whole worlds in which everything can be said and put in play without*

THE GREEN ROOM

JOHN HEJDUK

There are moments
that only time remembered
as when he brought
the rose to his lips
and the scent entered
his mouth
the red powder mixed
with his hearts blood
to enlarge the gray
veins near the surface
of his skin
his smile made
his cheek bones rise
and his almond shaped
eyelids slightly close
intensifying the silver
spheres of his pupils
floating in a pure white
porcelain liquid
his hands and fingers
were extremely long
he could imagine the hands
of the future Braque
his brushes beside him
they were centuries apart
Braque talked about
his paintings
Jesus listened
for he then knew
what was to happen
before he left
he arranged a bowl of fruit
into a still life
and painted a wood pear gold
a large purple bird
flew into the dark green room
then became enmeshed
in the arabesque wallpaper
Braque fell asleep in his chair
within his silence
he witnessed
the crucifixion of Christ

reserve, with the exception not of this fact but of the bot-tomless stake of the other world, I write by reconstituting the partitioned and transcendant structure of religion, of several religions, in the internal circumcision of 'my life'... I came up to write something else, for I come up now (into this loft, this 'sublime' to write" (10-14-77), I do not have the other under my skin, that would be too simple, the other holds, pulls, stretches, separates the skin from [*d'avec*] my sex in her mouth, opposite or above me, she makes me sperm in this strange condition, it's my condition, on this suspended condition that I write to death on a skin bigger than I, that of a provisional and sacrificed spokesman, who can't stand it any more, caelum *enim* plicabitur ut liber *et nunc sicut pellis extenditur super nos. sublimioris enim auctoritatis est tua diuina scriptura* [...] sicut pellem *extendisti firmamentum libri tui, concordes utique sermones tuos, quos per mortalium ministerium superposuisti nobis.* [...] *Cum hic uiuerent, non ita sublimiter extentum erat. non dum* sicut pellem caelum *extenderas, nondum mortis eorum famam usquequaque dilataueras.* / "For 'the heavens shall be folded together as a book,' and now it is stretched over us like a skin. Indeed, Thy divine Scripture is of more sublime authority [...] Just so, Thou hast stretched out the firmament of Thy Book like a skin, Thy wonder-fully harmonious words which Thou hast imposed upon us [...] while they were living here below, it was not so sublimely extended. Thou hadst not yet spread out the heaven like a skin; Thou hadst not yet broadcast the renown of their death in all directions" (XIII, xv, 16).

THE WALLPAPER

JOHN HEJDUK

Jesus saw that the large brown bird
was entangled in the pattern of
the wallpaper painted by Braque
and he was saddened by its plight
the painter was looking forlornly
at the wall
he spoke to the figure who had
entered and appeared in his room
you have come to see my paintings
I have come to release the bird
from your pigments
Lord let me mix you a color that
those on Earth have never seen
Braque did so
when Jesus looked at the miraculous color
he said to the old painter it is seen
in Heaven and now it is on Earth
Braque fell asleep in his chair
his long fingers held the brushes
he used to paint the color for Jesus
in the dawn when he awoke
the painted wallpaper
no longer held the bird in flight
in its place was a disc of the color
made in Heaven and Earth

TO JOHN HEJDUK

WHO DELIGHTED IN EDUCATING, IN PRAYERFUL DRAWING,
AND THE WRITING OF HIS OWN WILD PSALMS.

With profound thanks we celebrate The Silverweed Foundation and the Chanin Fund of the Irwin S. Chanin School of Architecture whose support assisted in the publication of this work.

WRITTEN WORDS

(pp. 10–26) "Poems" by David Shapiro, copyright © 2001 by David Shapiro. Used by permission of the author.

(pp. 30–56, and 58–87) *Journey to Poland* and *Letter from Regions of Delusion* by Michal Govrin, translated by Barbara Harshav, copyright © Michal Govrin. Used by permission of the author. First published in English in Partisan Review 1999/4.

(pp. 82–96) From "Circumfession" by Jacques Derrida in *Jacques Derrida* by Geoffrey Bennington and Jacques Derrida, translated by Geoffrey Bennington, copyright © 1993 by The University of Chicago Press. Used by permission of The University of Chicago Press. Originally published in French, under the same title, copyright © 1991 by Editions du Seuil.

VOICES

(pp. 11–91) Transcription of *Body of Prayer*, copyright © 2001 by David Shapiro, Michal Govrin, and Jacques Derrida. Used with their permission.

(p. 17) *Night Son Here* by John Hejduk, copyright © 1998 by John Hejduk. Printed by permission of the author.

(pp. 31–35, 49–55) From *Name* by Michal Govrin, translated by Barbara Harshav, copyright © 1998 by Riverhead Books, copyright © 1998 by Michal Govrin. Used by permission of Riverhead Books, a division of of Penguin Putnam, Inc. Originally published in Hebrew as *HaShem*, copyright © 1995 by Hakiboutz Hameuchad Publishers.

(pp. 95 & 97) From *Lines, No Fire Could Burn* by John Hejduk, copyright © 1999 by The Monacelli Press. Used by permission of The Monacelli Press.

THE HEAVENS SHALL BE FOLDED TOGETHER AS A BOOK

ה

Published in the United States of America in 2001
by The Irwin S. Chanin School of Architecture
of The Cooper Union for the Advancement of Science & Art
30 Cooper Square, New York, New York 10003.
All rights reserved under International and Pan-American
Copyright Conventions.

No part of this publication may be reproduced or utilized in any
form or by any means, electronic or mechanical, including photocopying,
recording, or by any information storage retrieval system, without permission in writing from the publisher. Inquires should be sent to The Irwin S.
Chanin School of Architecture.

Copyright © 2001 by The Irwin S. Chanin School of Architecture
of The Cooper Union.
Copyright © 2001 by David Shapiro.
Copyright © 2001 by Michal Govrin.
Copyright © 2001 by Jacques Derrida.

Designed by Kim Shkapich.
Printed and bound by Brodock Press.